REGENERATION.

By EDMUND H. SEARS.

"The existing state of Christianity amongst those who profess it does not warrant the objection, that all further advance in the development of the perception we possess of its nature and application is impracticable or unnecessary. If we *have* the perfect conception of Christianity, we are making a lamentably imperfect application of it; for the world, alas! is to a very small extent under its power; if we have *not* the perfect conception of it, then every attempt to regard it from a more lofty moral point of view should be welcomed as a real and earnest attempt for the highest welfare of mankind." — MORELL.

PRINTED FOR THE

American Unitarian Association.

FOURTH THOUSAND.

BOSTON:

CROSBY, NICHOLS, AND COMPANY,

111 WASHINGTON STREET.

1854.

CAMBRIDGE:
METCALF AND COMPANY, STEREOTYPERS AND PRINTERS.

NOTE.

THE following Treatise was written at the request of the Executive Committee of the American Unitarian Association, who earnestly commend it to public attention. As individuals, they may not concur in every opinion advanced, nor adopt every verbal expression employed by the writer, but they unanimously and cordially approve of the great thoughts and principles that form the basis of the work, and of the spirit and temper in which it is written. They publish it because they believe that the clearness and strength with which it states and enforces the great practical doctrines of Christianity, and the beauty and power with which it portrays and recommends the profoundest religious experience, will secure and reward a thorough study.

CONTENTS.

PART III.

THE NEW MAN.

INTRODUCTION.

No higher question can be offered to the human intellect, than that of the method of salvation by Jesus Christ. Its unmeasured importance is obvious to us, whenever in contemplative mood we open the pages of the New Testament, and find that a splendid apparatus of means has been provided; for we know that this would not have been done unless momentous interests were at issue. These two questions, What are we? and Whither do we tend? will at times press painfully upon thoughtful minds, and demand an answer. Ideals of a better state are haunting them, and producing within them unutterable longings after peace.

There are three topics which cannot fail to command the interest and attention of those whose minds are revolving the great problem of life: —

The evil, depravity, and suffering involved in the human condition; the darkness that broods upon the earth and upon our own spirits.

Conceptions of a better state; dreams of perfection, visions that come in shapes of unearthly beauty, floating out of a purer ether, and giving us gleams of a better world.

The way that lies out of one condition into the other, out of the darkness into the light, out of storms to the haven of Happier Isles; in short, the method of salvation.

These are the topics which we now approach, and we do it in the persuasion that they underlie all our business and all our theologies, and that, though they have occupied so much of human thought, yet they never pressed more urgently upon the common mind than now. The old theologies do not satisfy. They do not answer these questions. They do not so much give light, as hang in the way of it. And yet, because they are gradually changing and softening like convolving clouds, and reflecting new, though ever-varying hues, they show that the light is coming, and that they are finally to break away. Meanwhile let us use the light already shining, and that will be a preparation for more.

The theme we have in hand will lead us to discuss the following topics: the state of man by nature, his spiritual capacities, his regeneration and the means of it. If any of our reasonings should seem to lie remote from our beaten paths of inquiry, or if they should not sound like the traditional utterances of denomination, we would beg the reader to consider whether they may not be just as worthy of his attention. All sects are liable to fall into provincialisms of thought; to sink the language of the universal Reason into a corrupted dialect; and so it is better, if possible, on such themes as these to rise above sect and take our stand outside of it, haply if we may stand on those sublimer heights, where we may catch the clearer responses of the Divine word. In the following pages, therefore, we propose to leave behind the old controversies, except so far as to be intelligible, and so far as is necessary to show the truth in bolder outline by its juxtaposition with error.

Impressed with the solemn magnitude of these themes, we approach them in reverent and listening mood.

PART I.

THE NATURAL MAN.

THE ANCIENT DESOLATIONS; THE RUINS OF MANY GENERATIONS.

Isaiah lviii. 12.

"These are ruins indeed; but they proclaim that something noble hath fallen into ruin, — proclaim it by signs mournful yet venerable, like the desolations of an ancient temple, — like the broken walls and falling columns and hollow sounds of decay that sink down heavily among its deserted recesses." — DEWEY.

CHAPTER I.

THEORIES.

"If our native propensities are themselves a sin, then the conclusion seems to be plain and inevitable, that God is the author of sin; not merely that he has made beings who can commit sin, but that he has made beings a part of whose very nature, as it comes from his hands, is sin. . . . . . I am unwilling to plunge into the yawning gulf which is laid open by such a process of thought." — PROFESSOR STUART.

THE actual state of man by birth and by nature is a question still involved in the controversies of the schools. To turn aside to these would divert us from our main object; and fortunately this subject can be taken out of the province of polemics, and brought to the test of sober fact and reality. We will only allude, then, to the theories of the sects, so far forth as to give precision and completeness to the argument. With some variety of statement and confusion of coloring, where different creeds shade off into each other, we shall find in the main that the prevailing theologies on this topic fall asunder into three forms.

The first form is this, — that man comes into being burdened with hereditary guilt, inclined to all evil by the original bend of his faculties, and capable of no good until God by a sovereign act creates him anew. But lest we should misrepresent this form of belief, we prefer to state it in its own language, which lacks nothing in strength and clearness. The Westminster divines say: —

"The covenant being made with Adam, not only for himself, but for his posterity, all mankind descending from him by ordinary generation *sinned in him* and fell with him in his first transgression.

"The sinfulness of that estate whereinto man fell consists in the *guilt of Adam's first* sin, the want of original righteousness, and the corruption of his whole nature, which is commonly called original sin, together with all actual transgressions which proceed from it."

Another standard of faith states the doctrine thus: —

"By this sin they [the first parents] and *we in them* fell from original righteousness and communion with God, and so became dead in sin, and wholly defiled in all the faculties and parts of soul and body.

"They being the root and by God's appointment standing in the room and stead of all mankind, *the guilt of their sin is imputed*, and corrupted nature conveyed to all their posterity descending from them by ordinary generation.

"Every sin, *both original and actual*, being a transgression of the righteous law of God, and contrary thereunto, doth in its own nature bring *guilt* upon the sinner, whereby he is bound over to the wrath of God and curse of the law, and so made subject to death, with all miseries, spiritual, temporal, and eternal." *

* Ratio Disciplinæ. Confession of Faith, Chap. VI.

We confess to a shudder of the nerves when copying these words, which we do chiefly to make our statement exhaustive. We are apt to confound truth with error under the fog of indefinite language. It is a great deal better to lay them side by side, stripped of all the fine gauze which a more modern fastidiousness would weave around them, that each may be seen in its sharpest individuality. Then Christians would better understand each other, and the unwary would not be beguiled.

We find a difficulty in framing an argument against the theory of man here drawn out. An argument starts from premises that are self-evident, and proceeds to conclusions that were not. But we could not start with any thing more obvious than the axiom, that no man is guilty for what took place before he was born. We could not get back to any premises more self-evident than the absurdity which these propositions start with. They begin where reasoning generally ends. The result of a *reductio ad absurdum*, which generally comes out at the end of a demonstration, they put at the beginning as a truth assumed. How unprofitable, then, this whole controversy! How much better for the parties rather to cease from their logic and examine in a friendly way their logical machinery, if perchance they may find whose it is that is so out of joint, that in the moral calculus it refuses to give the result that two and two make four!

There is another reason why it is not worth while to enter on this branch of the subject. Pleasing omens already indicate that this form of belief is ceasing to become active. We lay it off, then, in the persuasion that it is taking its place among the fossilized remains of a former theologic world, which old convulsions had turned up and left bare to our wondering and curious gaze.

There is another view which may briefly be stated thus. Men, as they now come into the world, are in the same moral state in which the first man was created. His sin affected no one but himself; and human nature is not changed by the fall. The farther we trace the stream of life towards its beginning, the purer we find it, and with every one it is perfectly pure at the period of infancy. Man's true culture, then, is the development of his powers from within outward, under such external aids as this probation affords. What is corrupt comes to him from without, from wrong education, from vicious example, from the influence of a bad state of society. He starts in life entirely disconnected with the past, and has only to choose the good or the evil that is offered him.

This theory of man, which "cuts the thread of history from behind us every hour," is here stated very nearly as it came from the lips of its reputed framer,* and with some modifications and additions it has maintained its integrity for ages in the progress of human opinion. Its history has run nearly parallel with that of the doctrine first described, perhaps

* See the account of the system of Pelagius, Murdock's Mosheim, Vol. I. p. 371.

sometimes borrowing from it a darker tinge than its own, or a clothing from its mystic phraseology. May we suggest that it is a survey of human nature only upon the surface, without sounding its mystic and troubled deep? Hence those who adopt it so often recede from it as the mysteries that lie within successively reveal themselves. Hence a church formed around this as one of its central principles will seldom retain that class of minds whose habits of thought are ascetic or introspective, or whose deep and surging sensibilities demand some potent voice to guide and to soothe them, some light to explain their dark and terrible on-goings. Its recruits come from the side of the world; not from those who had before left it, and are passing on to deeper experiences.

The first theory so merges the individual in the species, that he is there lost and buried in one solid and gloomy mass of corruption, and the sin of one man was the sin of all. By the last it is resolved back into that extreme individualism which admits of no unitary life, but makes it exist in fragments or in endless and independent atoms. Does this last meet the facts of history, of consciousness, of revealed truth, better than the other? Does it meet the demands that come up from the profounder depths of human nature itself? We shall see, while, having done with the negative side of the question, we now advance to the positive.

CHAPTER II.

HEREDITARY CORRUPTION.

"Though all animals be fitted by nature for the life which their instincts teach them to pursue, naturalists have learned to recognize certain aberrant and mutilated forms, in which the type of the special class to which they belong seems distorted and degraded. . . . . . And now, in the times of the high-placed human destiny of those formally delegated monarchs of the creation whose nature it is to look behind them upon the past and before them with fear and mingled hope upon the future, do we not as certainly see the elements of an ever-sinking state of degradation which is to exist for ever, as of a state of ever-increasing perfectibility to which there is to be no end?" — FOOTPRINTS OF THE CREATOR.

THERE is a distinction, obvious to any one, between original sin and original *propensities* to sin; between hereditary guilt and hereditary evil. Man is guilty for what passes into wrong action through his free volitions; for what is wrong in his volitions, but not for what is wrong in his original structure. He is guilty, not for the wrong dispositions he inherits, but for the wrong dispositions which he admits into his own voluntary life; not for the depravity that was innate, but for the depravity that passes into conduct. His original moral constitution, whether good or bad, he could not control any more than he could control the color of his complexion; and he is no more responsible for the one than the other. Hence the obvious distinction between a nature which is *sinful* and a nature which is *depraved.*

Putting theories aside, we now come to the stern facts of experience and history. We must take these, not as we would have them, but as we find them. Hereditary sin or transmitted guilt is an idea which cannot be conceived without conflict of thought, or expressed, but in terms of self-contradiction.

But transmissive dispositions, and proclivities to evil, coming down along a line of tainted ancestry, and gathering strength and volume on their way by every generation that transmits them, is a fact that is universal, and so an irreversible law of human descent.

In unfolding the evidence of this proposition, let us commence with statements of a general nature, which challenge universal assent, and whose truth is open to the eyes of all.

What, then, is the actual condition of the race? Taken in the mass, it lies in spiritual darkness, each generation receiving from the past its gloomy superstitions and horrid idolatries. A race in its true condition, not less than a family or a state, would form a certain organic whole. It would be a family of nations, society in its grandest form, and that a form of beneficence, taking up every people and every tribe into one circulatory system of benefits and blessings, that poured life and happiness from all to each and from each to all. Diplomacy, trade, commerce, would form a grand system, that kept girdling the globe with charities, or perhaps rather the arteries and veins that kept sending life into all the members, and bringing it back. Instead of this, the nations and peoples are fallen asunder; we debate whether they belong to the same species; each is parted off to its solitary darkness and its bloody customs, and they present the spectacle of the fragments of a mighty ruin.

But survey the fragments themselves, and what do we find? Each organized around its favorite falsehood, or else disorganized altogether, as is the case with the savage tribes. They present the spectacle of class preying upon class, the weak lying as victims to the power of the strong. If you choose to except the Christian nations, which are no exceptions at all, yet remember that three fourths of the world lie under the night of barbarism, and need, not merely improvement, but re-creation out of chaos. And let us remember that the mission of Christianity was not *development*, but *reconstruction.** Its history would show how slowly the work is done. A distinguished statesman of the last century declared that the history of nations was a record of wrongs, and that the offices of kindness which one nation had rendered to another would not fill ten pages of its annals. The signs of a better day which now appear would mitigate, but hardly reverse, his judgment.

Now we must not look exclusively at the individual virtues that bloom out among every people. We must survey human nature through its grand organizations, and accept the fact that evil and wrong are not functional, but organic also. And we must also

* Isa. lx.; Rom viii. 19–22; Isa. lxviii. 12.

remember that we are surveying a race of which we ourselves are members, and that our judgment is exposed to the sway of its corruptions. Could we rise out of it, and survey it from a point outside; could we look down upon it with an angel's eye, from some mild-beaming and sinless planet, and take into one view the bloody march of its history, though we might not say with Mr. Burke, that this earth is the "bedlam of the solar system," we should certainly allow that it lay in wickedness, and that we surveyed the moral ruins of an apostate world.

Passing on to a view not quite so general, we come to the fact that the human species fall into divisions of races, and that each race has its own peculiar life and type of character descending through innumerable generations. Time, culture, and physical environments exert their plastic power within a certain range; but during three or four generations, and, indeed, during any known historical periods, *they never break up the type.* The origin of races is a question from which we retire. It is all the same, as regards this argument, whether the streams of migration first radiated from one or from many centres. We simply point to the fact, that each bears along its own qualities and colorings, which do not disappear through series of ages; that they become more distinctive in their divergence, and cut their channels deeper as they flow. The African is torn from his native groves, and driven through every variety of clime and fortune, but his ancestral life he never loses. The cold of Canadian hills does not freeze it up. The fire of tropical suns does not melt it out of him. The Jew floats on for ever, an element in the world's population, which all its attritions cannot break in pieces, nor its fiercest surges dissolve. Let art and civilization cover up this ancestral life under fairer forms and shows; let time file away its rougher features as man emerges out of barbarism, and then let the old temptations encircle him anew, and the old spirit will sweep through him and reappear. Refinement of manners and national comity will give way before it like threads of gossamer. A desire for his neighbor's lands was the unappeasable greed of the Anglo-Saxon and his cognate tribes, emerging grimly out of the Cimbric forests, and pouring successive waves of conquest over England. After the lapse of a thousand years, its motions are beating over the Mexican and the Sikh, in a resurgent wave of the same barbarism.

When a nation is composed of the same race, and is therefore homogeneous, a national life and national character become developed, the most intense and distinctive. Individuals become members of the same collective body, thrilled by its pulse, and marching to the same drill. They form one medium for the same mighty spirit which sways the individual, as the music-master touches to one tune all the strings of his lyre. Nor does it make any difference when its master minds disappear from the earth, except that the national life becomes still more deep and intensive. As if they departed only to come nearer on the spiritual side, and breathe on the souls of the living, they become its gods and heroes, and live in its history and its songs. The past is alive in the present, and common vices and virtues are perpetuated, and stamp the same lines on individual character. The same hatreds descend from parent to child, increasing in rancor on their way. If the common life is prevailingly corrupt, the corruption will thus channel its bed deeper and broader, till the last barriers break away. It destroys the organization through which it acted: the nation's life is consummated: it falls in pieces, and perishes miserably from the face of the earth. This was the "progress and termination" of the Jewish commonwealth, and all its neighboring nations.

But we suppose that the educationists of a certain school might here say, This is all the result of bad example and influence; take the youth out of this corrupt society, and from amid those unpropitious circumstances, and all would be changed. Waiving now the question whence *originated* this corrupt society and these unpropitious circumstances, we will only say that it would be exceedingly edifying to see this notion brought to the test of experiment. Let the educationist take the babe of the Bushman, and rock him in a New England cradle and a New England home, and see if a New England character would be produced as his natural faculties unfold. We do not say that he would grow up the same being that he would in his native society, under the recreative agencies that now act upon him; but whoever denies that the instincts, biases, and impulses of his tribe would surely appear and enter as an indestructible element into his character, denies what every naturalist knows to be true. The outward man even to the body, the most external clothing of the spirit, is shaped and moulded in some sort by the faculties that lie within. And this holds not of mere feature and expression, but of the whole internal structure of brain, nerve, and muscle, making the entire human form the exponent of the soul. The ancestral spirit, by a sort of elective affinity, appropriates the matter and form that shall fitly configure and manifest its own peculiar life. So that the naturalist, as soon as he looks on the human form, though it be that of the sleeping child, knows the race, and sometimes the tribe and family, to which it is to be referred; and he knows, unless some powerful countervailing agencies come in, the forms of domestic and social life, including customs, manners, art, worship, in which the spirit within will seek embodiment and exercise. The ancient tendencies have the moulding of us, then, before we are born. In their book "all our members are written." They shape and tone the finest tissues of our mental, moral, and physical structure, ere yet we have seen the light. So that the infant bears the stamp of his lineage, and is himself the configuration of the old ancestral spirit. Where a race is on a course of degeneration and moral decay, we see it in the forms and features of the youngest offspring. Where there is purity, intelligence, and celestial love, they put on the forms of masculine dignity, womanly grace, and those early spiritual charms that beam out from within all conscious and personal attainments; but there are tribes of men of whom just the reverse is true, and where humanity recedes and sinks down through the whole scale of brutal deformity, where what is manly is almost lost and what is brutal almost alone appears, where the brow retreats away, and the lower features project forward, which the lowest appetites and fiendish passions have made their own disgusting image.

All violations of the divine laws, as they pervade our entire constitution, tend not only to individual ruin, but *the degradation of species.* The tribes to which we have just referred hold a relation to the whole human family, such as monsters and idiots hold to the particular families in which they are born. Malformations of mind and body are referable to preëxistent infractions of these laws, and sometimes many generations intervene between the causes and their ultimate and dismal results. This is a law of transmission through all known grades of being. It is not peculiar to man, but it runs along the descending scale of all created natures below him. It underlies all the phenomena of reproduction, growth, and decay. And the malformation ranges through the vast interval between the first slight distortion from the fair and symmetrical original, to where the distortion is complete in monster individuals of a family, or monster families of a species.*

* See an interesting chapter in Miller's Footprints of the Creator, on the degradation of species.

If we narrow down our sphere of observation from races and nations to private households, we get illustrations of the law of descent which are familiar to all. The resemblance which was general becomes more and more special till we come down to single families. How notorious is the fact, that the peculiar mental, moral, and physical qualities of the parents are coined anew and expressed in the features and toned in the temperaments of the children! When children of the same family have been separated wide asunder, and the streams of migration have diverged into regions having no intercommunication, and the modifying influences of climate, marriage with other families, and diversified occupations have been at work two hundred years, still we have known the stranger pass from one region to the other and point out the common descendants before hearing their names. Thus habits of mind become inwrought and infibred with the natures of offspring. And thus fearful are our responsibilities, for such is the poison or the healing virtue which we infuse into the stream of being that sweeps by us. According to the life within which we choose to cherish and manifest, we leave an inheritance of blessing or a cleaving curse to the generations!

Scarcely less in form and feature than in language are the transmissive qualities and dispositions of a people to be discerned. Language is never an assemblage of arbitrary signs among the people with whom it is native and living. It is the crystallization of their most interior mind, and it shows the most peculiar colorings of their thought and sentiment fixed and preserved. Hereditary dispositions not only shape the features, but the vocal organs; and they give them that tone, compass, texture, and flexibility, whereby they shall prepare for themselves an appropriate utterance. They form their own gamut, and then they rise and fall through it as they will. They shape the human lyre for their own use, and then they sweep it with their own music. We know that every animal species is born into the instinctive use of a natural language, whose signs are uniform from age to age. Just as true is it that the same propensities in men will seek the same expression, and pre-adapt the organs to every shade of meaning, and that these organs are touched by the hereditary life and toned by the ancestral spirit, — for it is spirit that appropriates matter and moulds it and makes it flexile to its uses. Hence those who have strong mental and spiritual affinities soon learn and speak each other's language; but let the children of a people long savage and brutalized be taught a language flexile to the higher sentiments, and then be left to themselves. They will most assuredly sink such a language into miserable barbarisms, which, though not cognate with their own tongue, shall be allied to it in sound. For it is not they that speak, but a line of foul ancestry is speaking through them. The missionaries, when translating the Bible into the tongues of native savages, put the best Christianity into those tongues that they will hold. It is curious sometimes to render back literally, and see the Christianity *that comes out of them.* Let our educationist take the youngest child of the Polynesian savage, and teach him to speak with "pure tone" the dialect of mercy. Or if he can find a lineal representative of a tribe of the Northern forests, whose language Pritchard says "resembles the cries of wild beasts rather than the sounds of the human voice," since bestial passions so long had growled through its gutterals, let him train his larynx at once to vibrate to the soft sounds and the breezy motion of Tuscan airs. Scripture saith that the primitive men had first one language and "one lip." But they "travelled from the East"; they left the golden regions of that love by which human thoughts and sentiments are fused together and find harmonious utterance, and the primitive language was resolved into jangling dialects, each the howl of some selfish passion, — like a strain of many parts breaking down into discords, when each is glad to withdraw his part from the general clang. And hence the dispersion of ancient and of every modern Babel.

CHAPTER III.

ACQUIRED INSTINCTS.

"It might be sufficient, perhaps, to state the well-known fact, that dispositions and propensities, and consequently all *habits* that have acquired the force of these, are actually transmitted to descendants." — KINMONT'S NATURAL HISTORY OF MAN.

WE suppose that, if Pelagius were to rise from his repose, he might bring an objection somewhat on this wise. The facts which have now been stated do not prove any innate depravation of human nature. All its propensities are in themselves good. They only become depraved through voluntary perversion and abuse. The senses are all good, and even the animal appetites and passions. Things in themselves good may be used either for good or evil purposes. Appetite is for self-preservation, desire for property is to excite to industry, combativeness to defend the right, reason to investigate truth, and reverence to worship God. If in their perversion they produce licentiousness, avarice, murder, sophistry, and superstition, the fault lies in the use and not in the possession, and so all that is in man is originally good and pure.

If the traveller, musing amid the splendid ruins of Palmyra, should see in the broken entablatures, and tottering porticos, and columns half buried in rubbish and sand, the city of the desert queen in its primitive glory, his imagination, we suppose, would be deemed somewhat fertile and illusive. All that he sees in itself is good and beautiful, and once formed structures through whose halls passed a train of joyous beings, or around whose domestic altars clustered the virtues and charities. All the parts of those structures may be there still, but not with their original *adaptations and symmetries*, and that makes all the difference between a city in its splendor and a city in its ruins.

Man loses none of his faculties in the process of his deterioration, but he does lose their original symmetry and harmony. There is a certain relation between sense and reason and affection, which makes man's mind the fresh print and copy of the Creator's. There is that distortion, or complete *inversion*, which makes it the image of the demon's. Sense may serve the reason, or reason may be the subject of sense. Affection may be placed supremely on God or on self. The faculties may be toned and harmonized, and move in heavenly order, giving a sense of that wholeness and complete unity which exist in the Divine nature. This unity may be broken up, and hence there may arise the sense of inward conflict, as if nature by some dire convulsion were riven asunder. Human nature, to be transmitted in its purity, must be transmitted not only with all its original powers, but in its divine proportions and harmonies. If it comes with the sensuous powers developed into monstrous and morbid action, and the reason shorn of its brightness, it is a nature darkened and distorted, and therefore depraved.

Dr. South thus nobly describes the understanding of man in paradise: "It was then sublime, clear, and aspiring, and as it were the soul's upper region, lofty and serene, free from the vapors and disturbances of the inferior affections. In sum, it was quick and lively, open as the day, untainted as the morning, full of the innocence and sprightliness of youth; it gave the soul a full, bright view into all things, and was not only a window, but itself a prospect." The reason, in its sinless and crystal clearness, receives into itself the images of heavenly things, as the limpid lake receives and copies the overhanging scenery. But as man sinks lower and lower into the outward, he loses the power of spiritual sight and intuition, and when darkened and buried under the foldings of sense, immortality becomes, not a *perception*, but a *tradition*. The light from within and from above is shut out, and the external world alone is real. The mind gropes after truth, through the painful steps of a darkling and a drudging logic, on its "dim and perilous way" through the mazes of error, of doubt, and denial. Hence came the necessity of a revelation from without. It was not necessary when reason was a clear glass that mirrored back the skies. But when the "inner light" sank down amid the vapors and disturbances of the inferior affections, till it ceased to shine clearly, and the feet stumbled on the dark mountains, revelation came with its outward signs. Christ appeared with the power of miracle, — evidence addressed to the senses, since into sense men had so grosssly fallen, — and while it shows the Divine condescension, it shows in just the same degree the fall and the distortion of the human powers.

But there is another fact which is a full answer to the objection we have in hand. Though man loses none of his original faculties, — since in that case he would cease to be man, — he does acquire new and corrupt tastes and impulses, and these in their turn become transmissive. This is a fact as well known and established, not only in respect to man, but all species that have the power of reproduction, as any other fact in natural history. There are certain *acquired instincts* that perpetuate themselves, and change the habits, and sometimes degrade the race, in that line of descent. Not to write out a chapter in natural history, let the reader consult to his satisfaction the interesting section of Pritchard on that subject.* It is a well-known fact, that the vice of intemperance is propagated in this way; the diseased appetite descending from sire to son as a baleful heritage of corruption. As a single fact often weighs more with some minds than a volume of argument, we are tempted to relate one which comes on authority that cannot be questioned. A drunken parent had several sons, all of whom, with one ex-

---

* Natural History of Man, Sec. VIII.

ception, fell into the same degradation as himself. That son maintained his virtue, but the conflict was long and fearful. The depraved appetite which he never indulged, followed him and tormented him as if the word "rum" was rung by some demon into his ears. Resistance at last silenced the demon and drove him out. Such force is there in a human will when fortified by the spirit of God; but when the barrier gives way again and again through a series of generations, the tide of corruption gathers volume and velocity till it sweeps the barriers before it like rushwork, and the whole nature is given up to desolation.

But there are depraved affections and tempers, witnessed on a yet wider scale, which can never belong to an untainted moral constitution. The instinct of self-defence we will not arraign; but *pleasure in the infliction of pain*, which is the essence of all cruelty, and which fills the world with mourning, is the sure mark of a nature branded with the curse of Cain. It is first seen in the child who tortures the insect for his pastime, or who roams abroad, not to rejoice in the happiness that gushes from fields and groves, but to murder God's innocent creatures and mangle them in pieces. It is seen among men in that love of war for its own sake, which constitutes the very soul of murder. The business of war is entered upon, not as a work of horrible necessity, but as a work which affords a certain class of acquired instincts their keenest relish. Its art is contemplated with pleasurable emotions not less lively than those of the sculptor when breathing over his work the prayer of Pygmalion.* There are powers in man which need only to be restored to their first symmetry and order. The acquired and demonizing instincts of cruelty and revenge, need not to be restored, but purged away.

The history of every acquired instinct would disclose three distinct stages of development. There is, first, the transient emotion which ebbs and flows. Then there is the fixed mood of mind into which it settles down, when it operates an organic change in the moral, and thence in the physical structure. And, lastly, there is the altered constitution reproduced in the offspring. Anger at first is a flash of fire. Anger hoarded up becomes hate, and it settles into the brow and grates through the tones of the voice. Love at first may be an emotion that comes and goes. Then it is a fixed principle, beaming out of the heart so as to transfigure the whole person, and create a new face under the ugliest features. And the aversions of hate or the appetencies of love often appear in the next generation, in the transmitted feuds of families and nations, or in the heavenly inheritance of that good-will which was the burden

---

* "I ordered the artillery to be posted on a hill near the town and overlooking it, and open its fire. *Now ensued the most beautiful sight conceivable.*"

"The storming of ——— was a magnificent spectacle. *What a glorious feeling of elation took possession of my soul at that moment.*" — Livermore's *War with Mexico*, Chap. XXVI. — But see the literature of war *passim*.

of the angel-song. The first two stages in the natural history of the passions, we witness daily in ourselves or in those about us, — how evil passions run down the nerves and shake them out of tune, till the whole frame, though once like an organ of sweet stops, will discourse nothing but janglings and discords, — how corruption out of the heart will flood the brain and darken its "chambers of imagery," and thence derange all the vital functions of soul and body. Or, on the other hand, how pure affections, passing into high, rational, and spiritual frames, transform the whole man and create him anew; how benevolence works its changes from within, and makes the outer clothing of the spirit to be radiant and white as the light; how faith lays the soul to rest in the arms of God; how hope, from its first fond flutterings at the heart, changes into confidence and trust, when "wings at our shoulders seem to play," and bear us away from care and trouble into an atmosphere which is bracing and serene. He who denies that these opposite states of mind, after becoming fixed and habitual, affect the natural tempers and dispositions of offspring, shows that the simplest guardians of the nursery might teach him wisdom. Hence the path of endless progress that opens upward into light, or of endless deterioration that slopes downward into darkness and death.

CHAPTER IV.

TESTIMONY OF CONSCIOUSNESS.

"It is not what my hands have done
  That weighs my spirit down,
That casts a shadow o'er the sun,
  And over earth a frown
It is not any heinous guilt,
  Or vice by men abhorred;
For fair the fame that I have built,
  A fair life's just reward, —
And men would wonder if they knew
How sad I feel, with sins so few.

Alas! they only see in part,
  When thus they judge the whole;
They cannot look upon the heart,
  They cannot read the soul.
But I survey myself within,
  And mournfully I feel
How deep the principle of sin
  Its root may there conceal,
And spread its poison through the frame,
Without a deed that men can blame."

HENRY WARE, JR.

"It is no more I that do it, but sin that dwelleth in me." — ROMANS vii. 17.

THERE is a large class of minds, ranging through all nations, sects, and ages, which, though differing in their theologies, have a singular agreement as to the facts of consciousness. They draw various conclusions from these facts, but they bear uniform testimony as to the facts themselves. The testimony is substantially this, — that some evil forces within, lying deeper than their personal volitions, or acquired tastes, and antedating all their culture and habits, are seeking to possess and to sway their faculties. They give to the individual the feeling of divided consciousness. And this feeling is stronger just in the degree that the religious experience becomes more deep and vital. The more the interior man is searched and laid open by the word of God, the clearer are the demonstrations of this divided consciousness; and it seems to the individual that two classes of powers are ranged in opposition and seeking for the dominion of his nature. This conflict, perhaps, did not appear except under the light of Christian truth bursting on the soul in clearer splendor, — like the sun rising on a field where hosts are gathered and arrayed for battle, but which lay in stillness on their arms until the morning light should appear. Those who live a life merely natural, and outwardly blameless, yet who have never brought the most interior life under the judgments of the eternal law, have no such experience as we here describe. But it is conspicuously displayed in the lives of such men as Luther, Fénelon, Taylor, Bunyan, Fox, Edwards, and Ware, and the more so as the interior nature emerged out of dim twilight into open day, where all things appeared, not *in mass*, but *distributed*, and with their shape and quality confessed. Now the question may be raised, whether those moods be healthful or morbid, and whether the facts of consciousness are here rendered truly; but the question will hardly fail of a right answer, if we remember that oftenest out of these moods has come a robust and fervid piety, oblivious of self, earnest for great deeds and sacrifices, and with words that speak most effectively to the condition of sinful men. Yea, what mind penetrated with religious ideas has never been resolved into this same double consciousness, however dimly? Has the reader never, in the stillness of meditation and earnest introspection, had revealed to him the breadth and the purity of God's law, shining down into his soul as the serene almighty justice, and searching out all that was in opposition to itself? And in that all-revealing hour has he not been prompted to exclaim, "I am a man of unclean lips, and I dwell among a people of unclean lips, for mine eyes have seen the King, the Lord of hosts"? Has he not then seen a law in his members, warring against the law that shines down into his mind, waking up the old conflict which Paul has described in such living language? — God's voice calling one way, and a tide of inclinations and a throng of fancies sweeping the other way, which will not return nor subside at his bidding, — opposing powers, impersonating themselves in him and calling and answering to each other? Then he verifies anew the language of Paul, no longer a paradox, — "What I would, that do I not, but what I hate, that I do." Some mighty power is standing behind his personal volitions, and bending and swaying his faculties at its will, so that he does not seem so much to act and speak himself, as to be acted through and to be spoken out of. "It is no more I that do it, but sin that dwelleth in me." And what is the meaning of all this, unless it be that this sea of being, out of which we rise like bubbles out of some mighty deep, has its under tides and currents, whose force and swell have increased from remote generations, and they break into our consciousness, and we tremble with their motions and struggle against the downward rush of the waves?

CHAPTER V.

CHILDHOOD.

"Shades of the prison-house begin to close
Upon the growing boy."

THERE are two classes of qualities which appear in infancy and early childhood. There is the sweet smile of innocence, — the beautiful play of natural affection as it jets forth in a thousand fantastic shapes; natural sensibility, clear and gushing as spring-waters; imaginations white as falling snow-flakes, and whose furniture is yet unsullied as that of an angel's dream. Not that these are the uniform characteristics of this early age, but that they are very common, none but a cynic will deny. In what light they are to be regarded as elements of character and indications of the real state of man by nature, is a topic which we waive for the present, as belonging to another branch of our subject.

But to select these as the only characteristics of childhood were surely as uncandid as it would be to select the opposite ones and ignore these, and, like Calvin, compare children with vipers and serpents. If, as we have already seen, hereditary qualities are wrought into the mental, moral, and physical organization of offspring, and appear in the earliest form and features and make them the effigy of themselves, then we should expect to find inborn tendencies and biases to evil among the earliest manifestations. And so we do. Those beautiful traits are set within the ugly and depraved ones, and often overlaid by them, so that their beauty goes out for ever. That anger, deceit, irreverence, stubbornness, cruelty, and selfishness, in many a hideous form, are qualities which show themselves so early and with such entire spontaneity as proves them to be innate and hereditary, none, we take it, but dreamers will deny. And that they are developed out of the infant being, and not put into him by bad example, that they appear among the best encircling influences of home, and before example good or bad could be felt or understood, is a matter of daily experience. How often is it found that a sweet and sunny spirit is enshrined in an evil temperament amid biases to every wrong,— a rose that opens beneath overhanging briers that spring up and choke it and shut out the light till it dies away!

Even when the first manifestations of infant life are all pure and lovely, it is no sufficient argument to prove the absence of hereditary damage and disorder. The human soul is a germ whose unfoldings are to go on through the infinite ages, and not till its development proceeds apace are all its hidden tendencies brought to light. The blight and the canker may lie concealed when the first leaves disclose nothing but health; nay, the reason why the disease does not at first appear often is, that it lies so deep. How many are the foldings that are wrapped about us!—nature within nature, life within life, each to wake up and put forth its power, as the objects of temptation shall warm them into activity and draw them forth by their attractive charms. Around the spirit of that little being who slumbers in the cradle, there is a sensuous nature which includes the ovaries of the worst of vices, but which do not even give intimations of their existence until the dawn of manhood. Passions are there, coiled up and sleeping, which never yet have stirred, but which one day may strike their serpent fangs through that tender bosom. There is the possessory instinct, early grasping for what is not its own, out of which will come avarice with its sordid train. There is revenge, that thirsts for blood. There is the lust of the flesh, that will grovel in the sty of sensuality. There is the pride of life, with its empty pomps and glittering shams. There is cunning, that will seek its end by serpent windings. There is the lust of power, that will tread out humanity under its feet and "shut the gates of mercy on mankind." All are there, and if no re-creative power shall infuse healing virtue and restore heavenly order, these hidden forces shall surely come forth and be dramatized on the face of the earth, and ravage it in their terrible outgoings. All culture superinduced from without, all mere education, will have no other effect than to furnish these propensities with more keen and polished weapons to do their work. For education (*e-ducens*) is the leading out of these terrible armies. Left to themselves, they might rush out in savage disorder. A skilful hand may marshal them into exact discipline and brilliant array, not for private crime, but for speeding the bloody march of an unchristian civilization, or the consolidation of its oppressive power. And this is all.

From the fact that the evil spiritual forces which come down from the past with cumulative strength develop themselves only at successive stages of individual history, that they often lie concealed and bide their time, it results that men are often impelled into crimes which surprise even themselves, when some new field of temptation awakens the latent depravity, and the fearful mystery opens up into the consciousness for the first time. Hence, too, a prophetic eye sometimes reads the deep things of the spirit and sees its frightful history unrolled while the external man seems fair. The prophet looked into the face of Ahaz, then a blameless young man, and turned away and wept. Visions of ravaged kingdoms rose before him. All that Julius Cæsar was to be, was in like manner open to the eye of a sagacious Roman, when to the common eye all was patriotism and generosity. "Take care! there is many a tyrant and usurper in the person of that young man."

Those transmissive qualities of the human being which at first are latent, and whose activities are prospective, are revealed, or at least illustrated, in the physical man, which is the effigy of the moral.

It is a fact too familiar to be controverted, that the first years of infancy and childhood open ofttimes with the bloom of health and the promise of a vigorous manhood. But by and by the hereditary taint appears. The growth of the body unfolds the lurking malady, and the death wrapped up in a show of life appears. So families, and even tribes, perish from the earth, under the cumulative corruption which the stream of being in that direction bears along. The years of the generations grow less and less. They dwindle to a span, and then to nothing. They fail from the ranks of humanity, and leave only their names and their graves. And the man who should reason from first appearances in the cradle or the nursery against this stern law of human descent, would reason just as soundly as he who should deny the spiritual death included within the too transparent disguises of infantile innocence and beauty. For there are many innate propensities which do not show themselves until the carnal nature unfolds and warms them into conscious existence. The babe shows not the diseased appetite of drunken progenitors, but the surroundings of temptation may stir it up in the man. Nay, it may assert itself with perfect spontaneity, and with no external excitements. There are men of bland and gentle manners in private life, who will say, that on the field of battle, with the measured march of numbers, the martial music, and the presence of a foe, no sight is so lovely as that of falling and bleeding ranks, no work so sweet and genial as that of murder. The young of the tiger, it is said, may be domesticated, and for a while made mild and docile; but the first taste of blood will rouse all his native instincts; and his eye turns to fire, and he bounds in fury to the jungles!

CHAPTER VI.

THE MYSTERY OF DEATH.

"Fair daffodils! we weep to see
You haste away so soon;
As yet the early rising sun
Has not attained its noon.
Stay, stay,
Until the hasting day
Has run,
But to the even-song,
And, having prayed together, we
Will go with you along.

"We have short time to stay as you;
We have as short a spring;
As quick a growth to meet decay
As you or any thing.
We die
As your hours do, and dry
Away,
Like to the summer's rain,
Or like the pearls of morning's dew,
Ne'er to be found again." — HERRICK.

DEATH is described in all languages as a monster and anomaly in the universe. It is the kingly terror, the sum of all the agonies which afflict human nature. Where is the path on which its pale shadow hath not rested? Who does not remember the time when the stern fact of mortality broke in upon the gay fancies of his childhood, as the one giant sorrow for which there was no consolation. It would seem, sometimes, from the prevailing tone of our religious literature, as if the principal office of Christianity were to pour light and consolation over this one province of calamity. One would think, from much of our preaching, that the chief motive to religion was the fright that comes from this haunting spectre, whose approach must be made the dread of all our pleasant places. It is the "last enemy." It is the "cup of trembling." It is the "*ultima linea rerum*," — the dread boundary of joyous existence.

This calamity is peculiar to man. The inferior tribes know nothing of it. They obey the laws of their life, and so they have no dread of what is to come. The lamb gambols alike through the green pastures or to the place of slaughter. Up to the last flutter of her wings, the bird ceases not to trill her matins upon the air. But the only immortal being upon the earth lives in dread of death. The only being to whom death is an impossibility, fears every day that it will come. And if we analyze the nature of this fear, and explore the cause of it, we shall not be at all certain that it will not follow the mere natural man into a future life, and have an important part in its retributions. Man fears death only because he has lost conscious communion with Him in whom alone is immortality. In so far as we preserve our relation to Him who is the soul of our soul and the life of our life, our spirits wear the bloom of everlasting youth, and no more than the joyous child do we dream of consumption and decay. When this is lost, no matter in what stage of our being, whether in this life or another, we feel our weakness, we seem to lie at the mercy of change, and to hang over the abysses of annihilation.

And how mysterious are the shapes in which the spoiler appears! He comes not like an angel of peace, but seizes his victim as his prey. He comes in a grisly train of diseases and sufferings, the seeds of which the infant brings with him into the world. Yes, the infant that never knew sin has the tender fibres of his frame torn by the destroyer, and the death-agonies are received with the very boon of existence. Womanhood fades away in its beautiful prime, before its swift day has "run to the evensong," and manhood fails amid the heat and burden of the noontide hour, and the impress of suffering is left upon its glorious brow. Not one fourth of the race attain to the period of natural decay. One half, it is computed, die during the periods of infancy and childhood.

Can it be said that a human nature which has all this inheritance of disease, suffering, and mortality, has the soundness of its primal state, and that no taint has fallen upon it? We do not argue that mortality is the effect of sin, nor do we believe that the primitive man would never have died if he had never transgressed. But we do argue that death could never become this monster in the universe, could never make this train of diseases and agonies the grim heralds of his presence, could never make the human frame a rack of torture and turn its vital streams into currents of fire, unless something had perverted the fundamental laws of our being. We are surely treading here amid the ruins of a disordered and a broken nature. There is nothing in the fact of mortal change, which is merely outward and phenomenal, the flux and reflux of being on its course to the highest development of life, — there is nothing in this fact that it should be draperied about with mourning in our homes and churches. We look out at this moment into the natural world, and we there see the processes of death going on under very different conditions. There is something soothing beyond description, when nature puts on her death-robes, something which disposes to calm and holy musings. How peacefully does it come over the landscape, and what brilliancy does it fling upon the woods of autumn! And as we look along the western horizon, where "parting day dies like a dolphin" whom every ebb of life imbues with a fresh glory, what a contrast have we in the aspect with which it comes to nature and to man! We do not put these analogies in an argumentative way, any farther than to suggest what death might be, and what it would be to an untainted human nature. This flesh which we wear is the foliage of an unseen and an immortal life, and there is no reason why it should not fall away in its season, still and peaceful as autumn leaves, that this interior life may flower forth anew in the glories of unending spring. There is no reason why it should not steal on the decaying senses without a pang, so that while the mortal fades away, the immortal appears, one waxing as the other is waning, every entrance into the spirit-world being with a train of light lingering on the mind, sweet and mellow as that which rests on the hills at eventide.

But two things there are which barb the sting of death. There is this inheritance of disease that we speak of, — of organizations with broken laws and the earnest of swift decay. Hence death is not the unclothing of the spirit, but the rending away of its garment by violence. But more than this; man becomes buried in sense and matter, and this world becomes all in all. This world is the substance, while the spirit-world is the shadow. This is real, while that is spectral. Therefore to leave the solid earth is to tread away into nothing, and drop into the cold depths of the night, while on the ear from all that are loved and loving are falling everlasting farewells. On account of this seeming annihilation, nature sends up a deep and bitter cry. Or perhaps one sees before him the shadow-land which tradition has peopled with terrors, and where only phantoms are gliding past.

To a human nature in the freshness and purity of its morning prime, when celestial beings stood on the confines of both worlds and sang "strains suitable for both," the eye of faith would be open and clear; the spirit-realm would be the substance, while this would be the shadow; from infancy to age human beings would live in conscious fellowship with the sweet societies of the blest; death would come in his season, not to tear them away, but to lift a veil from their eyes, and disclose to them that sphere which already had sent its peace into their hearts and left its brightness on their souls.

CHAPTER VII.

THE "ADAM" OF ST. PAUL.

PAUL, in his letter to the Romans, has a passage which has figured largely in our theologies, and on account of its deep philosophical import we will cite it at length, in as literal a rendering as it will bear.

"Wherefore, as by one man sin entered into the world, and death by sin, and so death passed upon all men, for that all have sinned. — (For until the law, sin was in the world. But sin is not imputed where there is no law. Nevertheless, death reigned from Adam to Moses, even over those that had not sinned after the likeness of Adam's transgression, who is the type of him that was to come. Yet the free gift again is not so as is the offence. For if through the offence of one the many be dead, much more the grace of God, and the gift which is through the grace of one man, Jesus Christ, hath abounded to the many. Neither is the gift so as it was by one who sinned. For the judgment was of one offence to condemnation, but the free gift is of many offences to justification. For if by the offence of one, death reigned by one, much more they who receive the abounding grace and gift of justification shall reign in life by one Jesus Christ.) — Therefore, as by the offence of one judgment came upon all men unto condemnation, even so by the righteousness of one the gift came upon all men to justification of life. For as by one man's disobedience the many were made sinners, so by the obedience of one shall the many be made righteous. Moreover, the law entered that the offence might abound. But where sin abounded, grace did superabound; that as sin hath reigned unto death, even so might grace reign, through righteousness, unto eternal life, through Jesus Christ our Lord."

The Apostle's style is so exceedingly concise, that we must paraphrase his language a little in order to make it clear. He is arguing with a supposed Jewish objector; his style is interlocutory, and if the ellipses were supplied, his argument would proceed thus: —

OBJECTOR.

The blessings of the true religion are the peculiar inheritance of the seed of Abraham, and in the keeping of the Jewish Church; how, then, can Christianity be true, which breaks down sacred distinctions, and takes every body into its favor?

PAUL.

I reply to that, that a true religion has for its object to bring a remedy for sin and make men holy, and the remedy must be coextensive with the evil. Wherefore, as by one man sin entered the world, and death by sin, and so death hath passed upon ALL MEN, for that ALL have sinned. As sin was in the world before the Jewish law, so, therefore ——

OBJECTOR.

Pause. Sin is not imputed where there is no law. How can there be transgression where there is no command to be transgressed?

PAUL.

By the admission of your own Rabbins, death is the effect of sin. But does nobody die but Jews? Were men immortal till the Jewish law was given? Death did reign from Adam to Moses, even over those who had not, like Adam, transgressed any positive command. And this Adam represents the Messiah in a most important particular, — that the universality of the evil brought in by the one corresponds to the universality of the blessing offered by the other. Yea, the blessing transcends the evil, and in that respect they are unlike. For if through the offence of one the many be dead, much more the grace of God and the gift which is through the grace of one man, Jesus Christ, have *abounded* to the many. The grace not only remedies the evil, but gives a surplus of blessing beside. And in another respect the gift is not like the bane. For the judgment came through *one offence* to condemnation, but the free gift is of *many offences* to justification. The pardon is offered, not only to that one sin of Adam, but to all the sins that followed after. For if by the offence of one, death reigned by one, much more they who receive the abounding grace and gift of justification shall reign in life by one, Jesus Christ. Therefore, as I was first saying, as by the offence of one, judgment came upon all men unto condemnation, so, since the remedy is coextensive with it, the free-given gospel comes to all men unto justification of life. For as by one man's disobedience the many were made sinners, so by the obedience of one shall the many be made righteous.

OBJECTOR.

Admitting all you say, what need of the gospel? Make the law universal, for that makes men righteous.

PAUL.

Just the contrary! The effect of the law was that sin abounded more, for it revealed a perfect rule, but did not supply the grace to bring men up to its requirements. Not so of the gospel, for under that, where sin abounds, grace doth superabound; that as sin hath reigned unto death, even so might grace reign, through righteousness, unto eternal life, through Jesus Christ our Lord.

1. In what way physical death entered the world by sin, will be quite evident from the way that Christianity proposes to abolish it. The evil will be apparent from the nature of the remedy; the state

from which man fell, from the state to which he is to be restored. Christianity does not propose to do away the *fact* of man's transition from the natural to the spiritual world, but rather to do away with all the death-like environments which it now has. Those being removed, death is growth; the growth of man into the angel, amid the falling away of the hindrances and clogs of the inmost, the immortal life. It proposes to restore his nature to its primal order, to bring a fair and goodly creation out of its chaos, and then the inclosed immortal will break away from its integuments, not by the agencies of disease, but of superabundant life unfolding from within outward, casting off the natural body and assuming the spiritual, just as the covering of the worm falls away that the insect may rise with spangled wings into the air. This is not death, but health and life for ever enlarging. So that the death which Adam introduced was not the fact of human mortality, but the dismal drapery thrown about it.

2. It is obvious to observe, on a careful analysis of the Pauline philosophy, how much more than his proper share of the evil brought upon the world, our common ancestor has been made to bear. Was ever the memory of man so wronged and abused by his children! So far from laying off upon him the whole business of man's fall, Paul does no more than designate how the work began, and how sin was first introduced. His successors kept adding to the work which he only commenced, and death

passed upon all men, not because Adam sinned for them vicariously, but in that ALL HAVE SINNED. He sinned, and there, alas! *began* the work of the degradation of his species; the balance between good and evil began to dip the wrong way, his successors kept adding to the weight, sin became more facile with every generation, till the scale came heavily down. And this is THE FALL OF MAN.

3. Hence the Adam of St. Paul is not merely an historical person. He is only so treated in the foregoing extract, in order to keep up the antithesis between him and Christ. Not so when he applies his doctrine and appeals to individual experience! There it is the *Adam of consciousness.* It is the "old man," which is to be "crucified" within us, or which is to be put off as corrupt, in contrast with the new man, which is the ingenerated and indwelling Christ.* So then the Adam of St. Paul in this connection is a corrupt past, which has become immanent in the present. It is an inherited, disordered nature, impersonated in each individual. With primitive man began the descending series, and it kept on till the time of Christ. Then the ascending series began, and it will keep on till it comes up to the level of that height where began the march of humanity. Or to seek an image which perhaps will give us at once the Apostle's unclouded meaning: He regards the race in its totality, as an organic whole, as making one orb of being. With the first

* Rom. vi. 6; Eph. iv. 22; Col. iii. 9.

man's sin it began to dip into darkness, and the line of shade encroached upon it till it hung in disastrous eclipse. With Christ its emergence began, and it will continue till it rolls in complete glory along the latest ages.

CHAPTER VIII.

THE LAW OF DESCENT BENEFICENT.

"No one generation linking with the other, men would become little better than the flies of a summer." — BURKE.

WE suppose our argument will not be regarded as complete, unless we vindicate the justice and beneficence of the law of human descent, which we have endeavored to illustrate in the preceding pages. It will be said, that it does not comport with our notions of a just creator thus to burden his children with hereditary evil; that, after all, it is punishing the sons for the crimes of their ancestors, and is thus open to the objections to which the old dogma of original sin lies exposed.

A first and obvious answer to all such reasoning is, that the objection is merely theoretic. It argues from our notions of God to what we think the facts ought to be, and thus sets at naught the first principles of induction. Better accept the facts as they are, as they lie all about us and within us. The problem of ages has been to reconcile the existence of evil with the Divine attributes; and evil that comes by transmission is no more irreconcilable with those attributes, than the evil that forms the sharp environment of our condition and crushes us from without. Perhaps the evil that is transmissive and comes from within is more consistent with our notions of the Divine mercy, since it is more subject to our personal volition and control. Be that as it may, it is our wisdom to learn our state precisely as it is, to know all the difficulties that beset us, and then we shall turn with more enlightened vision to the means of our deliverance.

But we go further than all this. We vindicate the law of transmissive qualities and proclivities as essential to the permanence and the very existence of society. Unless the peculiar genius and dispositions of parents were produced anew in their descendants, through successive generations, what would humanity present but a mass of heterogeneous and discordant atoms? Societies, states, and nations could not be formed out of them and perpetuated. Society is the collective man, having a unity of its own, existing not only in a given locality, but through indefinite periods of time; having, like the individual, a development of its powers from youth to maturity and age; having a work to do on the earth; having schemes of improvement to be formed and matured through a series of generations. In order to this, the peculiar loves, tastes, and aptitudes of the fathers must ever be produced anew; the past must ever live in the present; the spirit of ancestry must go down in unbroken line to a remote posterity. The children cherish the memory of the fathers, inherit their life, and take up the work they left to make it over in turn to a new generation. Thus, while the individual is weak, society is strong. The individual is ephemeral, but society is immortal. The individual can do comparatively nothing; society accomplishes works of skill and grandeur which are the wonder and the charm of ages. But suppose this law of descent were abolished. Let the fathers have no guaranty that they shall live again in the children. Let every man come into being with the thread of history cut from behind him, commencing an existence original and *de novo*, without the peculiar loves and aptitudes of his ancestry or his tribe, and society at once is resolved into a wretched individualism, with which all progress must stop for ever; and all the accumulations of past wisdom and experience must be lost in a hopeless and endless chaos. Suppose, for instance, the transmitted tastes and tendencies of the Pilgrim were to cease with the present generation in New England, and the next generation were to come upon the stage, not with the inborn *conatus* of ancestry, but each individual with his own original proclivities, like Frenchmen, Chinamen, or promiscuously what you please. The past two hundred years would be lost to the future, and the land would sink, as by a stroke, into primitive barbarism. Laws would only be formed for the exigencies of the present hour. Or rather, since laws are the collective will of a homogeneous population, law and statesmanship would cease alike for ever.

The law of descent in its beneficent operations is the grand principle of organization by which humanity rises out of barbarism into its loveliest forms of life and beauty. Around this are formed, first families, then states and empires, then races, then a humanity full and complete, organism within organism, with all their interdependences and interactions, each homogeneous in itself, and operating for the good of all, forming together a human race that develops all the forces of human nature, and reflects in every possible way the charms and glories of the Divine. Such may it one day become. And the law of descent is an ever-recurring security that society shall not be subject to violent and destructive changes. Like the individual, its improvement and renovation shall not break up the continuity of its being. Even if it be on a course of deterioration, it shall decline and be dissolved with the least possible of individual suffering and ruin. But let that law cease by which generation links to generation, without which there is no hearty love and reverence of ancestry, without which the fathers cannot live in the future nor the children in the past, and society, if it could exist at all, would be always in a whirl of revolution. Every reform would be a destruction and a re-creation out of ruin, if, indeed, there could be enough of elective affinity among the chaotic atoms for any reconstruction to become possible. Every important change would be by dissolving the fabric into "the dust and powder of individuality."

The law, then, by which dispositions, good or bad, become transmissive, is a wise and beneficent law, essential to the existence of the collective and social man. But, like all the laws of creation and providence, it has necessarily a twofold operation. On pure and holy natures it produces ever new accumulations of blessing. On natures whose laws are perverted, it produces suffering; but the suffering is necessary and incidental, to be controlled and overruled for abounding good to those who seek to be benefited thereby. The same providence seeks our final happiness and regeneration alike in the evil that lies around us and in the evil that follows us from behind. Whether circumjacent or hereditary, it is subject to that law of optimism which seeks the highest good of the universe and of every individual that lives within it. It may be demanded, perhaps, Why is not the good transmissive without the evil? As if the evil stood apart in tangible shape, without interblending with our whole being, and entering essentially into the complexion of all that we call character. There is no man who is one half good and the other half bad. The good and the evil modify and interpenetrate each other in endless combinations, and if one is transmitted, the other must be. The law of progression and the law of deterioration are one and the same principle operating under different conditions. That man is wise, who, untrammelled by baseless theories, how much soever they may please his fancies, shall rightly apprehend his own interior state, and shall be so trained and disciplined, both by the evil within and the evil without, that he shall be among that number at last who come out of great tribulation, with robes "washed white in the blood of the Lamb."

We rest here in the third general theory of man which we announced, — that transmitted dispositions and proclivities to evil, coming down a line of tainted ancestry, and gathering strength and volume the farther they descend, is a universal law of human descent. Objections, doubtless, may still be raised, such as that every soul is a fresh creation of God, and is therefore pure. Or, again, that the tide of corruption that comes from behind us and sweeps us away, destroys our moral responsibility. The first objection we do not think it worth while to entertain. It is fanciful and vague, and reasons not from facts that we know, but claims to set those facts aside from some imaginary psychology. To the other objection we are sufficiently sensitive, and we grant that it might be valid if the foregoing argument claimed to give the whole account of man. But it does not: and this objection will disappear in the light of any rational and faithful delineation of man's spiritual nature and capacities. We have described the disease, for it behooves us to know the worst, though it lead us among ruins that are mournful. We turn now to views that are auspicious and cheering.

PART II.

THE SPIRITUAL NATURE.

There is in heaven a light whose goodly shine
Makes the Creator visible to all
Created, that in seeing him alone
Have peace; and in its circuit spreads so far,
That the circumference, with enlarging zone,
Doth girdle in the worlds." — CARY'S DANTE.

"The SPEECH OF GOD which produces the works of creation is that immutable REASON from which they flow, and by which they are perfected, — not an evanescent voice merely, but a living energy, reaching to the farthest extremities of nature and the most distant ages. In this manner God speaks to his holy angels, but to them audibly: to us otherwise, on account of our grosser apprehension. But when we perceive through our internal ears some faint notices of this Divine Speech, we approach the angels." — AUGUSTINE, DE CIV. DEI, Lib. XVI. cap. 6.

CHAPTER I.

THE HOLY SPIRIT.

"That which we find in ourselves is the substance and the life of all our knowledge. Without this latent presence of the I AM, all modes of existence in the external world would flit before us as colored shadows, with no greater depth, root, or fixture than the image of the rock hath in a gliding stream, or the rainbow in a fast-sailing rain-storm. The human mind is the compass, in which the laws and actuations of all outward essences are revealed as the dips and declinations." — COLERIDGE.

THE spiritual nature implies two things. A spiritual world which exists out of man, and a faculty in him to put him in connection with that world, and apprehend its objects. It implies the adaptation of one to the other. The physical nature includes the faculties of sensation: but the faculties of sensation imply their objects, — the world of sights and sounds and fragrance; of skies, fields, and waters; a world which puts the physical nature in connection with itself, and unfolds all the sensuous powers. Even so there is the same correlative fitness of the spiritual man to a spiritual world, or else the term *spiritual nature*, as applied to human beings, would be a term without a meaning.

Let us now approach the subject of the Divine nature so far forth as to deduce the doctrine of Divine influence. There are two sources of evidence that lie open to us whereby this doctrine may come clear and living to our minds. There is a sure and safe analogy, and there are the vivid descriptions of revelation.

Man is created in the image of God, and so in man the Creator has abridged and copied out his own attributes. Were it not so, we could have no communion with the Eternal Father, any more than the beasts of the field or the clods of the valley. We could not even form any conception of the Divine nature, for we could get no ideas answering to the terms which describe it, and God would be unrevealed in the human and finite images which set him forth. For instance, if there be a trinity in God, there would also be a trinity in man, that likeness which a pencil of rays out of his own nature has made of itself and projected into time. And just so far as it fails of realization in the likeness and the copy will the words that describe it be *words* and nothing more. And so of the Holy Spirit. In man must we find the analogy that sets forth its nature, else the terms that describe it will be sounds that float idle upon the air.

We describe the human being from two points of view;—man as he *is*, and man as he is *manifested* in his doings;—man in his own person, and man in the spirit that is breathed out of it; in his intrinsic nature and in its daily and hourly outgoings; in his essential being, and in the functions it performs in the economy of life; in the powers that lie within him, and in the influence that goes out of him, and creates the moral atmosphere, the insphering life that affects all things that lie within it. There are those whose persons we have never looked upon, but whose influence abides with us, transforming our characters, and permeating all our trains of thought and feeling when least we are thinking about it. Indeed, man in his finite degree may be said to create a world out of himself. He is furnished with the rough material, the primal chaos, so to say, which he acts upon and transfigures by his own effusive energies. Nature and society furnish the material which he works with plastic power, and he leaves on them the prints of his genius, and imbues them with the colorings of his mind. According to what he *is*, is the quality and amount of the virtue that goes out of him, and he cannot cease to impart his peculiar life unless he sinks into the lethargy of death. His hand, feeble though it be, holds the "golden compasses" of the poet, by which he marks off a portion of the chaos that lies about him; and this circumference is filled, and to some extent is changed, by that life that never ceases to go out of him. Some modern philosophers would have us believe that its manifestations are more subtile than ordinary senses have ever detected, and that all things about him, when least he is conscious of it, are imbued and imprinted with his genius.

Indeed, this same distinction holds of all created things, — things as they exist in their own form and essence, and as they impart their virtue and perform their use in the grand economy, from the modest flower that rises by the way-side and exhales its sweetness on the ambient air, to the sun out of whose orb come the never-ceasing waves of glory that break on the outermost limits of the universe. Not a tree nor a leaf—no, not a clod nor a stone—out of which virtue of some kind is not always going. Not a substance which has not its attractive or repellent forces, and which does not impart either health or poison. Could we see into the life of things, we should know how they act and react upon each other in such wise as to elude our clumsy analysis, and that that grandest conception of the imagination had hardly outrun the sober truth of philosophy,—

> "There 's not the smallest orb that thou behold'st
> But in its motion like an angel sings,
> Still choiring to the young-eyed cherubins;
> But while this muddy vesture of decay
> Doth grossly close us in, we cannot hear it."

Ascend we now to the august conception of the Holy Spirit of God. The Divine Being exists in one infinite and glorious person, but out of that person comes the life that pervades the universe, and constitutes the latent principle out of which all other forms of life do blossom forth. It is the effluent energy that creates all souls in its own image, and which by never-ceasing effusions would make them beautify and grow towards its own perfections. Falling into mute and insensate natures, *they* are only moulded into the passive and unconscious images of the Divine wisdom, beneficence, and beauty. But falling into the natures of free and rational agents, and freely and rationally received, it produces love, wisdom, holiness, making man the active and conscious likeness of the supremely Good and Fair. Hence man returns the love he receives, and hence his *communion* with God. Free and spiritual beings may receive this influence in more full or more feeble measures, and so among them are all gradations of spiritual life. The sensual and the sinful grieve and quench the spirit. But it is received in more beatific measures among the inner ranks of saint and angel, and yet more by those inmost ranks that do always behold the face of the Father, —

> "The circles in the circles that approach
> The central sun with ever narrowing orbit."

Conceiving the true doctrine of Divine influence to be of primary importance, we must ask the reader now to put this conception of the Holy Spirit in contrast with some other views, that it may stand out with due prominence. We put it in contrast with the idea that the Divinity is an impersonal spirit that pervades humanity, or a blind unconscious force that rolls through nature. The idea of God is not to be confounded with that of the spirit which he sheds abroad. We know of no spiritual influence which is not the outbreathing life of a living person. We know of no spiritual power which is not the attribute of a conscious being. Out of man and above man, out of nature and above nature, is the Divine Person, around whom centre all the splendors of the Godhead, but from whom is that effluence of light and love which pervades the whole circuit of being, and makes every atom glow with his omnipresence. "Do not I FILL heaven and earth? saith the Lord."

Again, we put it in contrast with that abortion of the human intellect, the personality of the Holy Spirit, as we have not a doubt that this latter is the source of much that is anomalous in the prevailing modes of spiritual nurture. For if the Holy Spirit is a person that comes and goes between man and God, his advent will be hailed by tumults of rapture, his departure and absence will be bewailed as the era of desolation and mourning, his return will be sought by mystic rites and agonizing conjurations; the wildering fancy will see the signs of his return in its own wandering lights and irregular frames; the favored families which he visits will be pointed out, and the families which have been "passed over" will seem abandoned to perdition. The churches will increase rather by periodic agglomerations than by homogeneous and perennial growth. There will be the alternation of chills and fevers, not the consciousness of God's abiding spirit, always given, always immanent, and whose life is ever to be unfolded in the crowning virtues and graces of the Christian character.

CHAPTER II.

ITS GENERAL AND SPECIAL INFLUENCE.

"But when he came the second time,
He came with power and love;
Softer than gale at morning prime
Hovered the Holy Dove.
The fires that rushed from Sinai down
In trembling torrents dread,
Now gently light, a glorious crown,
On every sainted head." — KEBLE.

THE declarations of Scripture which describe God as acting upon man and working in man, naturally arrange themselves into two general classes. In the first place, they set forth the doctrine most distinctly and unequivocally, that God works in all men; that his is that universal and incumbent spirit by which all minds, whether Christian or heathen, discern a power above and within themselves, an everlasting law that lies upon them and seeks its realization in all their voluntary actions. This eternal spirit, whether transfused through nature and making all sensible things to copy out the eternal mind, or whether coming directly from within, has the same end, to woo the human spirit to itself. Paul places both Jew and gentile alike under condemnation, not only because the eternal power and Godhead had been revealed to the gentiles in visible things, but because he had been revealed in their own consciences and had written his law upon their inmost hearts.* And the same truth is brought out with amazing prominence in the steps of that divine argument comprised in the first fourteen verses of John's Gospel. That same Divine Word by which all things were made, and by which therefore visible things became the expression of God's mind, or, in Platonic phrase, the *pictures of God's ideas*, — this Word also came to man and shone amid the thick-folding darkness of his soul. "In him was life, and the life was the light of man, and the light shineth in darkness, but the darkness comprehendeth it not." It was that life enshrined in the inmost of humanity, and always in effort to shoot up its light into the human consciousness and bring man's life into harmony with itself. And because obstructed by those folds of sin and error which generation after generation had laid around it, this Divine Word became incarnate in Jesus Christ; God was manifest in the flesh, that the nations might *behold* his glory, since that glory was waning to its extinction in the soul.

"It is God which worketh in you both to will and to do of his good pleasure." † That man has the power of *originating* truth and goodness is one of the illusions of his own pride. His mind is not a machine, created and set agoing, to work out its results independent of its Framer. Rather is it an organ-

---

* Rom. ii. 15. † Phil. ii. 13.

ism for the reception of light and life in perennial streams from the Eternal Fountain, and by that life to grow for ever into a brighter image of God. Man is made such an organism by the very constitution of his spiritual being, and he cannot cease to be such unless he ceases to be human, and falls away from his species. It is on this sure ground that the Scriptures place the doctrine of human responsibility, in regard to those people who have received no special revelation. Even the material world would have been to the gentiles no revelation of the eternal power and Godhead, unless that same power which spread abroad its scenery had imparted his informing and imbreathing spirit to interpret its signs. So, then, every form in which humanity can possibly appear is an organism adapted to receive into its inmost nature this effluent life of God, just as in the natural world every thing that grows, from the daffodil to the cedar of Lebanon, is flooded by the light and heat of the sun, by which the vital juices are kept in motion, and out of which are woven the colors of woods and fields. All the spiritual graces which man puts on through the thousand shades of character, both Christian and heathen, are in like manner from the life of God received within and thence blooming outward upon the world. As soon as he receives existence, he receives along with it intellectual and affectional powers, one to receive truth and be formed thereby into the image of the Divine reason, the other to be kindled and guided by it and be formed thereby into the image of eternal love. There is no mind, moreover, into which hath not dawned the great idea of right and wrong, and that quivering sense of justice in all men which they call conscience, and which the Apostle says made the heathen a law unto themselves, is formed by the gentle and never-ceasing undulations of the Holy Spirit through the heart. Man lives in two worlds at the same time, one of matter and one of spirit. Not more surely do the external senses open outward and downward, and put him in communication with material things, than a finer sense opens inward and upward, through which come the idea of God and tidings of immortality. Not more surely do his sensuous faculties bring into his ear the sound of waters, and over his brow the breath of breezes, than his spiritual faculties admit to his soul the aura of heaven and the still and awful beatings from the heart of God. "What nation or race of men can be found," asks a heathen writer whose pages are more alive with spiritual ideas than much of our Christian literature, — "what nation or race of men can be found, which have not without any teaching some preconceptions of Deity, some idea of the subject by which the mind is *preoccupied*, and without which there could be no questions and reasonings about it? There must be divinities, for we have thoughts of them which are inseminated and inborn."* So he will have it that the primal truths are not the discoveries of man's painful logic, but they roll in upon

* Cicero, De Natura Deorum, I. 16, 17.

him from the all-informing Intelligence, and to perceive them he has but to listen and to pause. At any rate, we are shut in to one of two alternatives. We must assume that all the disinterested virtues, all godlike sentiment, and the ideas of God and immortality and the divine law, which are found outside of Christendom, are what man has evolved out of his own reason, independent of divine aid, and so he can be wise and good of himself, or else we assume that God is never without a witness in the hearts of all his rational creatures, and that the Eternal Word is the true light that enlighteneth every man that cometh into the world. We take the latter alternative, in company, as we think, with the Evangelist and the Apostle, and we say, as Erasmus did after reading Cicero on duty and immortality, "I am so affected that I cannot doubt that the breast whence such things proceeded was in some way occupied by the Divinity."

But while the New Testament writers assert this immanence of God's spirit in man, they use the words Holy Spirit in a more restricted sense, and as describing a special influence. The Saviour, on the eve of withdrawing his personal presence from his disciples, gave promise that he would send the Comforter, the spirit of truth, to guide them into all truth and bring all his teachings to their remembrance. Up to the hour of his ascension, they were ignorant of the nature of his kingdom, and the truths of Christianity lay dead in their memories. But after ten days had passed away, and while they were assembled at Jerusalem in expectation of some new tokens from on high, the promised influence came. God's spirit swept through their souls like rushing breezes; the truths that lie dead in their memories are blown into flame, their powers of utterance are unloosed, and such is the new light within that it seems to play around their persons like lambent fire.* This was the commencement of a new dispensation of the spirit, which ever since has been enjoyed by the Christian Church just so far as she has observed the condition of its reception. Yes, it was the great purpose of Christ in coming into the world to prepare the way for this new advent of the Divinity in the human soul. It was to remove all obstacles in the way of God's access to humanity, that he, who is always coming, might be always received.

Now it is important to observe, that this new divine influence differs in degree, though not in kind, from the universal action of God in man before described. Ever and everywhere the hindrance to this action is the sin and the ignorance of man, the dark and baleful cloud formed from exhalations out of his own heart, and hanging between him and the Divine glory. But for this, God would inundate our souls every hour with the warmth and the splendors of noon. Precisely here was the consummation of the mission of Christ. He came first with a dispensation of truth, and the dispensation of the spirit was the necessary consummation. He penetrated the

* Compare John xx. 26 with Acts ii.

darkness that brooded over the mind, and God shone without hindrance into it. And so the Church in the day of its purity appeared in an age of darkness, like one of those refulgent spots which lie upon the landscape under a riven cloud, and which on either side are flanked by the shadows flung from its wings.

All those passages of Scripture which describe the operations of the Divine Spirit, whether as a general dispensation to human nature, or a special dispensation to the Christian Church, are in strict harmony with the deductions of analogy. True, there are passages in which it is personified, but it is personified in just the same way as is every attribute of God, — his Word and his Wisdom, his Mercy and Truth, his Righteousness and Peace.* In its operation, it is always represented as the effluent life of God. Take its current phraseology, being "filled with the Holy Ghost," "baptized with the Holy Spirit," and try to annex the idea of a person, and the understanding is overwhelmed with confusion. Take the whole Pentecostal scene, where the spirit descended into the minds of the Apostles, and appeared around them like the play of nimble lightnings, conceive of it as a person, and your conception becomes perplexing and monstrous. But think of it as an influence from the one Infinite Person, which imbathed their souls with its tidal fragrance and light, and all is clear and rational, and in close accordance with the facts of Scripture and analogy.

* Ps. lxxxv. 10.

The new dispensation of the Holy Ghost, introduced through the mediation of Jesus Christ, is a topic to which we shall return when treating of the means of regeneration. What we now observe is, that it is the same Holy Spirit, the effluent life of God, of which all nations and ages have had some perception and experience. But by the mediation of Christ, it was made more operative in human redemption. Both the general influence and its special adaptations to the human condition imply a nature in man receptive of the gift.

CHAPTER III.

SPIRITUAL INFLUENCE.

"..... Of that innumerable company
Who in broad circles, lovelier than the rainbow,
Girdle this round earth with a dizzy motion,
With noise too vast and constant to be heard, —
Fitliest unheard! For, O ye numberless
And rapid travellers! what ear unstunned,
What sense unmaddened, might bear up against
The rushing of your congregated wings!" — COLERIDGE.

THE Christian believes that after the event of death he shall be transferred to a sphere of spiritual being, and be surrounded by the denizens of another world. But what if we are already in it! What if already we are environed by its "numberless and rapid travellers"! This veil of flesh that hangs about us is designed not more to reveal God to us, than to attemper and soften to us his intenser brightness; — to hide the stupendous agencies by which he sways us, and to muffle the noise of their footsteps, because our ears could not bear the too solemn sounds, nor our eyes gaze on the too beautiful sight!

Man, in the great plan of providence, is not *transferred* from one sphere of being into another. Rather is he brought into conscious relations to a higher and yet higher sphere, by the successive development of his original powers. The infant, first introduced into this world of sense, scarcely sees its varied forms of art and nature. All is a blank, or all is confusion; but he has within him a faculty which gradually unfolds and comes into exercise, and then what new and endless prospects open around him! The man blind from his birth has seemed to himself to live only in a very narrow sphere, through which he groped painfully, breathing the fragrance of fields and bathing in the warm sunlight, yet seeing not the objects whence they come. Some skilful hand touches the undeveloped faculty and removes its obstructions, and lo! without any transfer, he lives in a new world, that floods his soul with grandeur and beauty. He has not been carried into it, for it lay all about him before, and poured its influence upon him; but now for the first time his developed powers have brought him into open relations with it. Nor can we say how far this might still go on. Not one half of the glory and excellency even of this visible sphere has ever yet revealed itself to our dull senses, and agencies too refined and subtile for our detection are every moment playing around us and through us. Were our perceptions sufficiently quickened, or new perceptions given us, what a new world of wonders would open upon us, even where now we stand, transcending all our imaginations and dreams!

Even so the spiritual world is not a realm far off in space, into which we shall be introduced by the event of death. Rather is it that order of being of which we are to have cognizance by the powers that already wait within us, and death will not so much remove *us*, as remove *from* us the obstructions that closed us in from its unseen illuminations.

We read that sometimes in the plan of Divine Providence this inner sense, which ordinarily is not brought into exercise until that moment when the spirit is dissevered from the swathings of the flesh, is for special reasons opened before that time, giving to the prophet cognizance of those schemes and orders of being which surround him. The patriarch lay down to rest, and while his external senses were closed, this inward eye was unsealed and opened wide, and lo! the vast agencies are revealed to him, rank above rank, that "move up and down on heavenly ministries." The prophet is called to his solemn office while the coverings of sense are rolled away, giving him gleams of that sublime ritual by which the heavenly hosts waft praises to the Creator. The three favored disciples withdrew with their Master to the stillness of the mount, and there saw him as he appeared within the concealments of flesh and blood, holding converse with the glorified prophets. The Saviour passes from the scene of temptation to the scene of victory, beset in the one by the tempting fiends, and encircled in the other by the ministering angels. The great Apostle is for a time freed from the clogs of the body, and sees things which cannot be described.*

---

* Gen. xxviii. 12; Isa vi. 2; Matt. xvii.; iv. 1–11; 2 Cor xii. 4.

Now the question arises, Do these facts stand alone, or are they shining portions of a universal law, which in its all-circling operations has in these instances come into light? Are they special agencies, which in these cases have come and gone, or are they simply openings through the veil, that show to us what always is taking place? Was the spot where the patriarch slept indeed more holy than other places, and was the bush of Moses the only symbol of angelic ministrations? or rather, could we see as they saw, would not every spot be holy, and all nature seem aglow with those activities which run from the spiritual world into the natural? Was the Saviour of men our example in temptation only, or was he not also our example in victory, revealing to us those heavenly auxiliaries that work with us and strengthen us as we toil up the hill of Difficulty towards the regions of peace? And on the mount of transfiguration, was the change in *him*, so that he appeared as never before, or was it in his *disciples*, so that they saw him as he always had been, living in two worlds, walking on the earth and yet "the Son of man who is in heaven," talking with men and yet commercing with the skies? To our apprehension, these facts are not single and arbitrary. Indeed, no such facts exist anywhere, could we read them aright. When we call them single and arbitrary, we seem to forget that they presuppose those slumbering capacities that wait within us and the proximity of the sphere of immortality, and that our transit from this to that is only as "a sleep and a waking." Man could not be the subject of such revelations unless already he lived within the precincts of the mystic world, and had a faculty within him to be acted upon by its essential laws. These concealments of matter which engird us are therefore but frail walls that shut us in, which, falling down, give us sight of those higher skies that arch over us, and those brighter fields that lie around us trodden by the feet of angels, and over which breathe the airs of celestial love.*

---

* We trust it is not necessary to point out to the intelligent reader the distinction between that influent life which we suppose to come to man from a spiritual world, and open communication and intercourse with its inhabitants. The former comes to him internally, not falling into his consciousness as a distinct mental process, but falling in with all the natural processes of thought and emotion, to render them healthy and pure. Open intercourse with the spiritual world, on the other hand, is the applying of its agencies to the outward senses. The former, like the Holy Spirit itself, unfolds our powers *from within*, preserves us in freedom, and fortifies our manhood. The latter comes to us in dicta *from without*, and *may*, if yielded to, destroy our freedom and break down our manhood. The veil that hangs between the two worlds of spirit and matter was placed there as a protection and guard, because in our present state we cannot bear an open view of spiritual realities. It is obviously not in the order of Providence to give to any one an open vision of any other sphere than the one in which his works and duties lie. What is beyond or above this, we take hold of by another and a higher order of faculties than the senses, so that no disturbing sights or sounds shall sway or divert us. In those cases recorded in Scripture, where mortals have been suffered to look behind the curtains of Futurity, we shall find that it was not for *their* special benefit, but on account of the historical crisis in which they acted, and then under a special Divine protection. While, therefore, we have no wish to discuss at all those phenomena known as "spirit manifestations," but leave them to work out their own legitimate results, we yet rescue our

Are we touching this theme with too bold a hand? If it seem so to our sensuous philosophies, let it be borne in mind that we are interpreting, not only the word of God, but the latent convictions of the human heart, and that when the philosophers are at variance with those convictions which form the substrata of universal belief, the philosophers are uniformly at fault. What mean, not only these thoughts that wander through eternity, but the thoughts that wander from eternity into time, and lie on the common mind like a haunting presence, unless it be that the spirit-realm already inspheres us, and stirs our souls with strange feelings and anticipations? In those crises in the good man's life when darkness seems to brood over all his affairs, whence that communion which he has with the solemn troops of glorified saints, as if their faces shone through the clouds, and their conquering spirit had possessed his heart? Yea, is not the scheme of Providence itself a grand system of mediation? He moves on his vast designs,

---

own doctrine from perversion. And we would say, that we believe the higher world of spirits may yet so act upon our faculties *from within*, and so mirror itself upon the enlarged and clarified reason, that the objects of faith shall be quite as real to us as the objects of sight, and the inner realms and orders of being in which we already live, be imaged on the eye of our faith with a consistence and brightness that no external communications could give. Nay, further, we suppose it quite possible, that in this way we may come to apprehend spiritual laws and modes of being, while in the body, much better than many who have emerged out of it, and who, if they were permitted to speak to us, would give us, not laws of being, but disjointed facts, or fantasies without facts, and so only ply us with the gossip of their own sphere.

not only by his own direct influence and agency, but by those ministries which descend, one rank beneath another, to the lowest affairs, and link the least event with the greatest.

The spirit-world, then, is not far off. The good man with every new Christian grace is brought into holier affinities with the societies of the blest. The bands of angels come near and close around him, and when death uncovers his sight, it simply shows him where he is! More true is it than the writer himself intends who says it, that while his feet touch the earth, his head is "bathed in the galaxies of heaven." The bad man withdraws from those blest societies, and seeks alliance with the lost, so that when death opens his inner sight, it also shows him where he is; shows him the community of woe into which he has introduced himself, and the baleful scenery that lies about him. Every day do we breathe the airs of heaven or the blasts of hell.

When the first man saw the sun going down in the west, how might he have quailed at the thought that hopeless night and blank nothingness only were to follow. But it was the lifting away of that veil of sunbeams that did blind and dazzle him so that he could not see the vast creation in which he lived. The endless systems among which our little orb is interlocked by numberless bonds of attraction, and along with which it travels the celestial spaces with tremulous motion, would never have been known to us, unless the light that made us blind had been withdrawn, that we might gaze upon those giant wonders and glories. In like manner how does the deceitful glare of this earthly scene obstruct our vision! And how will the going down of its sun bring on, not the night we dreaded, but the vision of those vast orders of being to whose attractive power we had moved when we saw them not!*

---

* "Mysterious night! when our first parent knew
Thee, from report divine, and heard thy name,
Did he not tremble for this lovely frame,
This glorious canopy of light and blue?
Yet, 'neath a curtain of translucent dew,
Bathed in the rays of the great setting flame,
Hesperus with the host of heaven came,
And, lo! creation widened in man's view.
Who could have thought *such* darkness lay concealed
Within thy beams, O Sun! or who could find,
Whilst fly and leaf and insect stood revealed,
That to such countless orbs thou mad'st us blind?
Why do we then shun death with anxious strife?
If LIGHT can thus deceive, wherefore not LIFE?"

BLANCO WHITE.

"The glories I have described cannot be all. Shrouded by the veil of day, they would, had the earth, like the sluggish moon, turned on its axis only as it moves in its orbit, have been hidden hopelessly and for ever by the gairish beams of the sun. Yes, though their bright haunts are always around us, and, in virtue of the universal sympathies of things, play upon our beings unceasingly, through influences and laws not yet unfolded, even their partial and interrupted cognition by the human spirit flows wholly from a physical character of our globe which perhaps might not have been. Is it not possible, then, that, through other conditions of our conscious being, we are engirt by other universes, which, though at present veiled, — thinly it may be, — are yet real and vast as the world of stars? What are those dreamlike and inscrutable thoughts, that start up in moments of stillness, apparently as from the deeps, like the movements of leaves during a silent night in prognostic of the breeze that has yet to come, if not the rustlings of schemes and orders of existence, near, but unseen?" — NICHOL.

CHAPTER IV.

THE PRIMAL INNOCENCE.

"Dear child! dear girl! that walkest with me here,
If thou appear'st untouched by solemn thought,
Thy nature is not therefore less divine:
Thou liest in Abraham's bosom all the year,
And worshipp'st at the Temple's inner shrine,
God being with thee when we know it not." — WORDSWORTH.

WE have stated that the Holy Spirit is not a special agency that comes and goes at certain seasons, to be sought in frames and raptures, but that efflux of light and life out of the Divine nature, which pervades the whole orb of being, and becomes immanent in the human soul. We now proceed to the illustration of this truth, and to this end we select first for consideration the period of childhood.

We might well suppose that this would be pre-eminently the period when God would be around and within the little being, like an atmosphere of love. For not yet has hereditary evil been warmed into rank luxuriance. Its germination will come, alas! as soon as the influence of the world falls upon it, or as soon as its growth from within shall reveal the leprosy that is lurking there. But as yet its germs are quiescent, and when can God be so near to it, and when can those angels that do always behold the Father's face bend around it, as now, with the imbreathing fragrance of heaven?

But let us come to the facts, and let us read them aright. There are amiable qualities which in infancy are always more or less manifest, — innocence, tender sensibility, and unsullied love. They appear with entire spontaneity, as if a purer sphere were seeking to mirror itself in the crystalline spirit ere the motions of turbid passion have disturbed its limpid deeps. Along with these, ideas of God, of Right, and of Duty are awakened, generally with the earliest dawnings of the reason and the powers of language.

But it is said that natural innocence and gentle dispositions appear also among the lower species as mere animal instincts, and therefore they do not indicate personal holiness. We are not saying that they do. There are a great many things which are good and lovely, which do not indicate the presence of personal holiness. The creative energies of God flow down and manifest themselves in lower forms than man, even through all forms of animate and inanimate nature. There in lower types are copied out his infinite wisdom and goodness. The bird of morning, without knowing it, pours her matins to the Creator's praise. The lamb that gambols over the pastures, the dove that hovers around us on gentle and graceful wings, are natural images of celestial purity, innocence, and peace. Hence God's Spirit is called the holy dove, and Jesus is the Lamb of God. Not only so, but these same images are found in inanimate nature, — in the dews that distil softly as God's grace, in the winds that breathe, like his spirit, the invisible element in which all things live, in waters whose suffusions upon the brow symbolize the all-cleansing suffusions of God's spirit within. Now how do these lovely and beneficent qualities differ, as they appear in nature and as they appear in man. Just here, — that in nature they are the unconscious and passive manifestations of the Divine goodness and reason, while man has the power to discern their quality and receive and manifest them, *not in obedience to blind instincts, but in obedience to a Divine command.* Then he transmutes them from natural qualities into spiritual. They change their character when passing through the alchemy of a human spirit, and under the action of a human will. What else were natural amiability merely, is transfigured into the Christian graces and virtues. What was natural becomes spiritual, as water became wine at the touch of Jesus.

So then the natural innocence of infancy, though not holiness, any more than the natural innocence of the lamb, indicates, nevertheless, the preadaptations of the all-plastic Spirit to produce holiness. Those tender affections, and snow-white fancies, and guileless dispositions, in which during our infancy heaven lies about us, are soon to pass beneath the moral choice of a voluntary agent. He is to decide whether he will take up this heaven into his own breast and bear it away from natural things as his everlasting treasure, or whether it shall be lost and only remembered as the dream-light that reposed upon the hills of his childhood. So long as these qualities are merely natural, they are not his own. They wait to be appropriated. They may be wrought by him into his character as its essential elements, or when hereditary evil shoots up with tropic luxuriance they may be choked among the thistles and thorns. But how much is gained to us, that heaven is the first to mirror its eternal purities on our hearts and fancies, and that God's spirit is the first to enter the soul through its spontaneous motions! Even though these visitings be rejected, they may linger on the memory like a dream of paradise, so that the grace-hardened sinner shall seem to himself to have descended into a world of guilt out of a preëxistent state, "trailing clouds of glory" after him that were dissolved in the black night that finally shut him in, until, as it appeared in the visions of the opium-eater, he sees the towering gates of ingress at length closed upon him and hung with funeral crape.

It furnishes strong conformation, we might almost say absolute proof, of the view we are now taking of the state of infancy, that conversion is often produced by those tender voices of the memory, coming down through a long past, waking up the feelings of childhood, and making its familiar scenery rush back in vivid pictures upon the fancy. The lessons of parent and teacher are forgotten, and seem to have passed away. The docility of the child is gone, the effusions of infantile affection cease, under the hard incrustations of the world. But some incident calls them back, some great truth put home with a point that pierces the heart, some stroke of God's providence that shivers through the layers of indifference and sin, and lo! as by a magic wand, the burial-places of memory deliver up their dead, and they sweep in long procession down the desert of years; the best impressions of childhood revive with amazing freshness; the lessons long forgotten come back in the old familiar tones; the texts out of the old Bible preach anew; the prayers that went up from a mother's knee now plead afresh, nor plead in vain. The wanderer from home forgets a parent's blessing, and breaks his first resolves; he plunges through the doors of infamy, and crime has become so familiar, that the conscience is dregged and the sensibilities are turned to stone. But he goes back to the spot whence his wanderings began; the old hearth-stone is cold and the old faces are changed and gone, but the heart melts and the big tears of penitence roll fast upon a mother's grave.

There are two passages in the teachings of our Saviour in which this philosophy of conversion is divinely set forth. The young ruler came to him, inquiring what he should do to inherit eternal life. So much there was of amiability in the person of the young man, so much of natural goodness blooming in his countenance, so much of gentleness in his address, for he came to him kneeling, that the sensibilities of the Saviour are touched, and beholding him he loved him. But these qualities are only natural ones, and when the Saviour puts him to the test of voluntary obedience he fails.* Could we follow him further, how should we find that those graces which blossomed forth with such early promise faded away and disappeared, and that the amiable young man was changed into the hard and covetous Jew, not because those early qualities which put forth their spontaneous beauty were not good, but because they did not become fixed elements of character, through voluntary obedience! How often has this history been repeated before our eyes! And those qualities and graces, which in childhood are the living transparencies through which "the kingdom of heaven" shines down into the kingdom of nature,† are left behind, manifested in the spontaneity of the child, but not fixed in the voluntary life of the man. And yet repentance may bring them back; for we read of another who wasted his substance in riotous living, so that fain he would have herded with the swine. But he thinks of his father's house, sweet memories are stirring at his heart, and he "comes to himself." He goes back to the sunny spot whence his wanderings began. The scenes of his innocent days, that never ceased to haunt his visions, are given back to his eyes, and there, where he tended the flocks, and drove them afield, he weeps away his guilt on his father's bosom. ‡

We have seen an incident quoted from Audubon's Ornithology, illustrative of the principle which we

---

* Mark x. 17. † Matt. xix. 14. ‡ Luke xv. 11.

have in hand. It is found under his description of the Zenaida dove. "A man who was once a pirate assured me, that several times, while at certain wells dug in the burning, shelly sands of a well-known key which must be here nameless, the soft and melancholy notes of the doves awoke in his breast feelings which had long slumbered, melted his heart to repentance, and caused him to linger at the spot, in a state of mind which he only who compares the wretchedness of guilt within him with the happiness of former innocence, can truly feel. He said he never left the place without increased fears of futurity, associated as he was, although I believe by force, with a band of the most desperate villains that ever annoyed the Florida coast. So deeply moved was he by the notes of any bird, and especially those of a dove, the only soothing sounds he ever heard during his life of horrors, that through these plaintive notes, and them alone, he was induced to escape from his vessel, abandon his turbulent companions, and return to a family deploring his absence. After paying a parting visit to those wells, and listening once more to the cooings of the Zenaida dove, he poured out his soul in supplication for mercy, and once more became, what one has said to be the noblest work of God, an honest man. His escape was effected amidst difficulties and dangers, but no danger seemed to him comparable with the danger of one's living in violation of human and Divine laws; and he now lives in peace in the midst of his friends." *

* Quoted in the New Jerusalem Magazine, March, 1842.

We should even suspect the genuineness of that conversion which did not reawaken these spiritual states of childhood. It was produced, we should fear, solely by the terrors of hell, and not by the more sweet and tender calls of God's spirit, and the result would be the austerity of the bigot, and not the spirit of the child.* Such conversion is an angular turn in one's history, an arbitrary fact forced upon him, having no genial connection with his past and his future. All the past is rejected as worthless, and along with it the gales that come from the climes of morning, and "breathe a second spring." It is not so of conversions which are true and genial. As we journey from the East, we descend into the vale of shadows, but the regions of the dawn do not quite disappear. We still catch gleams of the golden sunlight on the orient hills. It is a most interesting and significant fact, that in that old age which is pious and serene, and in which the work of regeneration approaches its consummation, the memories of childhood are more distinct and vivid than of the long intervening years, so that the

* "Men laugh at the falsehoods imposed on them during their childhood, because they are not good and wise enough to contemplate the past in the present, and so to produce, by a virtuous and thoughtful sensibility, that continuity in their self-consciousness which nature has made the law of their animal life. Ingratitude, sensuality, and hardness of heart, all flow from this source. Men are ungrateful to others, only when they have ceased to look back on their former selves with joy and tenderness. They exist in fragments. Annihilated as to the past, they are dead to the future, or seek for the proofs of it everywhere, only (where alone it can be found) in themselves." — Coleridge.

extremes of life are brought into nearest relationship with each other. Even, then, if we lose sight of the spot whence our weary march commenced, yet when we climb the western summits and look back, that spot comes into view again; and though the space between were long and dreary, yet at the beginning and the end of our course are the peaks that jut out of time into eternity, in full view of each other and with the light of heaven playing on their summits.

We suppose no Christian doubts that the Saviour of men clothed himself in our weak and suffering nature, that, in all its weakness and all its suffering, sympathy and succor might come to it out of his divine compassion. He made the divine grace available to us in every possible stage of our pilgrimage. It is a question, then, well worthy the attention of those who think childhood is to be kept for future repentance, and is expected, meanwhile, to run into all kinds of depravity, whether Christ is indeed an all-sufficient Saviour, and whether his dispensation of grace is wide enough to span our whole existence? And why did he become not only man, but also a little child? Why did he "wrap the cloud of infancy around him," except that he might hold undisturbed communion with our "simplicity." Why, but to pass through the whole circle of human wants, desires, and sufferings, and take up every portion of human experience into his own, that no period or condition of life should be bereft of the aid of the great Mediator? How strange the notion, that, while he helps the mature and the strong, the helpless little ones he leaves as orphans! But no; the Dove's white wings also hover over them, and shed stainless glories upon them, and the Lamb of God, who taketh away the sins of the world, is especially with the infant and the little child to ensphere them in his own innocence and purity.

The Saviour declared of little children, that of such is the kingdom of heaven, and that whoever receives that kingdom must receive it as a little child. We quote the following, not only for its prophetic insight, but as the best exposition that we can find among the "commentators" of the Saviour's language.

> "Such hues from the celestial urn
> Were wont to stream before mine eye,
> Where'er I wandered in the morn
> Of blissful infancy.
> This glimpse of glory, why renewed?
> Nay, rather speak with gratitude,
> For if a portion of those gleams
> Survived, 't was only in my dreams.
> Dread Power! whom peace and calmness serve
> No less than nature's threatening voice,
> If aught unworthy be my choice,
> From thee if I would swerve,
> O, let thy grace remind me of the light,
> Full early lost, and fruitlessly deplored,
> Which at this moment on my waking sight
> Appears to shine, by miracle restored!" *

---

* See Wordsworth's incomparable "Evening Ode."

CHAPTER V.

LIGHT IN DARKNESS.

"Haunted for ever by the Eternal Mind."

THE spiritual nature in man, answering to the spirit-world to which he is destined, and in which he already lives, is hardly less perceptible in his most fallen state, than in his state of primal innocence. We will not say that he may not fall so low that the Spirit shall cease to strive with him, and the inward ear shall be deaf to the heavenly voices. The Saviour speaks of a sin against the Holy Ghost, in contrast with the sin against the Son of man.* The last might be forgiven, the first never. The careful reader of the New Testament knows very well, that the terms "Christ" and "the Son of man" are often used representatively for Christianity itself, or the system of truth which Christ embodied and revealed. The Holy Ghost, on the other hand, describes, as we have seen, an influence through man's inmost being, the pulses of divine life through the centre and core of his heart. The first is truth pre-

---

* Matt. xii. 31.

sented from without, — the other is the divine love that vibrates through the universal soul. Truth presented from without may be rejected, and yet one may be saved, for the error may lie no deeper than the understanding. Not so when the pulses of the divine life shall cease to beat within, for then the heart changes into the insensibility of flint, and nothing can melt it again. Therefore he who rejecteth Divine Truth may be forgiven, but he who rejecteth the Holy Ghost out of his heart hath no forgiveness, for he hath rejected the sovereign agency in his redemption. The first sin the Church has been swift to punish, while in more than one stage of her history, by killing that life out of which bloom the charities and humanities, she has herself, like the Jews of old, fallen into the last, most deadly of all heresies.

But these belong to that stage of man's history, or those periods of the world, where guilt reaches its culmination. They imply still, that man is an organized recipient of life from God, and that guilt and sin only in their ultimate results can destroy that last tender place in the soul, through which come the pulse-beats from the eternal love.

The state of worldly indifference is not a state of repose. The mind is tormented with ideals of a better state, and the heart is conscious of deep wants that are never satisfied. How could this be, unless the dreary present saw something in contrast with itself; unless the splendors of immortality let fall their struggling beams through the envelopments of worldly insensibility. They sleep, "perhaps to dream," and dreams of a bliss unrealized disturb the slumbers that else were the slumbers of death. Every sigh for a better life is the *Come up hither* of the glorious multitude, whose invitations fall down into the soul and rise up again in never-ceasing echoes. This could not be unless the mind opened inward towards a spirit-realm, and voices more than mortal talked along the solemn avenue.

Even the hardiest unbelief has those doubts and misgivings which come from the angel-voices that will not quite be driven out, or from that Divine Word which shineth in the darkness, though the darkness comprehendeth it not. Those who thought they had convinced themselves that the eternal Past and the eternal Future were regions of blank nothingness, and the questions Whence? and Whither? no other than if you shouted into a chasm, have found that some new experience opened unknown depths within them, and brought new faculties into exercise, and then beyond the chasm the Delectable Mountains rise clearly on the sight. Unbelief is seldom satisfied with its creed of denials, so that through its regions of desolation the pilgrim often travels to the most unshaken ground of his faith. How could this be, unless a spiritual world were already acting upon his spiritual nature? How could the spiritual faculties awake, whether they would or no, and give out the Memnon sounds, unless smitten with beams from other worlds, and made responsive to unearthly melodies? If the light comes not to bless and to save, it will come at awful intervals, like flashes of lightning at midnight, to make the darkness visible. Perhaps there is not a more significant passage in religious literature, than the suppressed passage of Mr. Hume, where he describes the influence of his speculations. He surveys the habitation which, with infinite logical skill, he has builded about him, and he starts with horror at sight of the gloomy and vacant chambers. "I am astonished and affrighted at the forlorn solitude in which I am placed by my philosophy. When I look about, I see on every side dispute, contradiction, and distraction. When I turn my eyes inward, I find nothing but doubt and ignorance. Where am I, and what? From what causes do I derive existence, and to what condition do I return? I am confounded with these questions, and I begin to fancy myself in the most deplorable condition imaginable, environed in the deepest darkness." The desolation and the emptiness are seen and felt, but they could not have been, except in contrast with a light too early lost, or by some star not yet gone down in the sky.

Not indifference and unbelief alone, but confirmed impenitence and guilt, are alike illustrative of the truth in hand. The darkness of the hardened transgressor is not solid and uniform. It lies between spaces of light. It is flecked with sunbeams, and because he will not follow the light, it only makes his night more baleful. What mean the forebodings that visit his pillow when this outward scene is withdrawn, unless at that hour the forms of another world are flinging their giant shadows upon his spirit? And what are the perturbations of his mind, but that which some one has finely described as the tremblings of the scale of Divine Justice? The Holy Spirit comes in showers of grace to those who welcome it and follow its light, but to those who do not, it turns to showers of fire. For the conflict in the soul of guilt is none other than hereditary and acquired corruption, seen and felt in awful contrast with the Perfect Law, the everlasting Right. This contrast could not be effected, unless the divine sphere of purity reached the soul, and produced the avenging consciousness of violated justice; unless some drops of divine light fell upon the conscience; unless the absolute law shone down through the soul, and shot through the moral nature the arrowy lightnings of remorse.

CHAPTER VI.

DISTINCTIONS.

"I am sure there is a common spirit that plays within us, yet makes no part of us, and it is the Spirit of God; the fire and scintillation of that noble and mighty essence which is the life and radical heat of spirit and those essences that know not the virtue of the sun, — a fire quite contrary to the fire of hell. This is that gentle heat that brooded on the waters and in six days hatched the world: this is that irradiation that dispels the mists of hell, the clouds of fear, horror, despair, and preserves the region of the mind in serenity. Whoever feels not the warm gale and gentle ventilation of this spirit, (though I feel his pulse,) I dare not say he lives." — Sir Thomas Browne.

It results from the foregoing argument, that there is in human nature an inborn capacity for goodness, virtue, and holiness, since by its very constitution it is made, from the beginning, receptive of the Divine Spirit, and opens inward towards the influence of a spiritual world. Hereditary corruption may gather around this inborn capacity, and human nature may be filled with the germs of all evil; still, through the inmost recesses of the soul God is always speaking, always operating, always waiting to be received. This is the strength which is always available to human weakness, this is the consuming fire which fills the souls of the guilty with corroding memories.

It will be seen at once, that this is a very different doctrine from that which gives to human nature original and independent powers for virtue and progress. Human nature is sometimes represented as capable of self-development, through its own separate resources. Or yet again, as a spark struck out from the Divinity, to shine ever afterward through its own unborrowed effulgence. Man, like God, has the power of originating truth and goodness, through the independent exercise of his own faculties.

We represent, on the other hand, that man no more originates truth and virtue, than the plant originates the sunshine in which it warms and expands. Like the plant, which is an organism to receive the light and the heat of the solar beams, and through them to be clothed in glories more rich and varied that those of the robes of Solomon, so the human soul is an organism to receive divine light and influence, and through that to grow into all the graces and glories of Christian excellence. If the light were put out in the heavens, all the beauty would vanish from the many-colored landscape, and darkness fall upon the fields like a pall. So if at any moment human nature were cut off from the Eternal Light, all the excellences and graces which make up the scenery of the moral world would vanish in uniform night.

We distinguish, then, between an original capacity for goodness and original goodness itself; between the power of originating truth and the capacity of receiving truth and being formed thereby into its resplendent image. And we hope to make it appear that this distinction is of such vital importance, that there is no true progress unless it be kept steadily in view.

Let one start, then, with the assurance that moral excellence is self-development out of an original fund of goodness deposited in human nature, the exercise of an independent faculty of his own. It results inevitably from this, that all culture will start from self and centre around it, and have self-exaltation for its object. It results just as inevitably, that all the pride of the natural man will be excited and developed, and intellectual culture and religious forms and ceremonies will serve alike to inflame its fires. The dignity of human nature will consist, not in its capacity to receive the Divine Image, as the placid and lowly lake receives the glowing skies into its tranquil deeps, but in its power of exhibiting a dignity and splendor out of itself, which resemble the splendors of the Godhead. The human soul will seem to itself a portion of the Divinity, and sufficient unto itself for all its progress and culture. Whatever virtues and moralities are put on, they are but the exhibitions of self; whatever be the forms of devotion, they are but the splendid liturgy that "wafts perfume to pride." These moralities and devotions will be lifeless, and they will only serve to wrap round and decorate the corruption of the natural man, a corruption that is never subdued and never removed. Hence there is so much of self-culture without self-renovation, so much of outward conformity where there is no inward life, so much of natural depravity that lurks under the vain disguises of Christian civilization. That which is God-given, man claims as his own, and turns to his own private uses. He steals the eternal fires. The virtues are his own; they come not from hourly acknowledgment and self-surrender. There can be no morality which shall be redolent of the divine life within, no regeneration, no worship that shall be any better than gilded mockery, until men in spiritual things as well as natural shall cease to violate the awful command, "THOU SHALT NOT STEAL."

In contrast with these ideas, and the culture which grows out of them, we put forward the doctrine that the Divine Spirit, though immanent in man, is not a part of man, not a separate faculty of his own. He may not appropriate the empyrean light, and claim it as his, for then the light being shut in becomes darkness, and the divine voice, being confounded with his own instincts, is changed into babblements and lies. On the other hand, the source of this Light must be profoundly acknowledged, and our daily dependence upon it. Then it stands apart in its awful sanctity and authority: we dare not steal it and appropriate it, but we bow before it in lowly surrender. Not self, but God, then becomes the radiant centre of all our thoughts. Conscience is not now a self-moving power, but a capacity through which a Power which is out of us and above us sends its eternal utterances into our inmost being, showing our own corruptions in mournful contrast with the Absolute Purity and Excellence. Then we do not attempt to bring down the Divine Spirit to the level of our own powers, but we suffer it to lift us up into the circle of its own radiance: we do not impress it into the service of our own interest and pride, but we suffer it to abase our pride, and we sacrifice all our interests to its behests. Then we do not confound its voice with the suggestions of our own passions, but we suffer it to cleanse away our passions and bathe our souls in its all-entrancing beauty.

Coleridge has somewhere described a man who used to take off his hat with great demonstrations of respect and deference *whenever he spoke of himself.* Perhaps there was more method in his madness than might at first appear. Let the idea of the Divine Personality be lost, and then God will be merged in nature or in man. The universal reason becomes itself the Divinity, and first obtains impersonation in individual men. So the creature's personal attributes become divine, and self-contemplation is the highest devotion, and self-worship is his daily ritual. Not the surrender of all his powers to the one Infinite Person to be shaped anew by its sovereign and plastic influence, but the exaltation of those powers to the place of God when most they need strength, and guidance, and renovation, — this becomes the characteristic of self-culture. Then one's own cognitions are the supreme authority and his own utterances the infallible oracle. "Ye shall be as gods," knowing good and evil, through self-illumination. And these are the gods from whose afflatus come confused prophesyings, which throw the world into bewilderment, or fill the air with the babblings of strange tongues. This is the religion for which the man in Coleridge instituted the most appropriate ceremonial. But the light within is not the scintillation of our own faculties, but the truth streaming in upon us from above, and claiming to be recognized and acknowledged. God did not create the human machinery and leave it to work out its own results. He CREATES us always in the present time. He works within us to will and to do of his good pleasure, on the single condition of self-surrender. This apprehension of man's relation to the Highest is calculated to beget in him that sweet sense of hourly dependence by which alone he is truly exalted, that self-abasement which comes of self-revelation, that state of hourly prayer whence rises to God the soul's unceasing hymn. The contrast which we present, therefore, is the contrast between self-exaltation and self-abandonment; between the arrogancy of pride and the grace of humility; between the attitude of self-sufficiency and the attitude of continual prayer; between a worldliness decked out in religious forms and decencies, and a piety that warms in the divine effulgence; between a worship that centres around self, and a worship that brings us lowly before God; between a soul that stands in the cold shimmer of its own vanities, and a soul clothed in the Divine Beauty as with rainbows.

CHAPTER VII.

TOTAL DEPRAVITY.

"How, it is inquired, are infants regenerated who have no knowledge either of good or evil? We reply, that the work of God is not yet without existence because it is not yet observed or understood by us." — CALVIN.

WE are not at all anxious to keep terms with the old theologies, much less to gloss over any real differences between falsehood and truth. But the terminologies of religion become so vague and so emptied of their primitive meaning, long before they fall into desuetude, that it is necessary to subject them to a clear analysis to see for what ideas they stand, or whether they stand for any. It is a fact very familiar to the historian of opinions, that an old system of theology may pass clean away, and a very different one take its place, without the least change in the old creeds and nomenclatures, just as the Roman republic passed into the empire, and liberty changed into despotism, without the least change in the *forms* of government. Nay, when men become secretly conscious that the ancient faith is leaking out of its symbols, it is quite observable how they cling to the symbols with a fiercer dogmatism, in order to elude the charge of innovation and heresy.

In this extreme anxiety to preserve the husks of dead men's thoughts, it may come to pass that those whose creeds are hostile may agree substantially both in opinion and sentiment. As it is not the husks, but their contents, that we care for, we wish to compare our doctrine with that which may be supposed to be current under the term "total depravity."

We classify the internal forces of human nature under a threefold division. Under the *first* division we place those which are evil in themselves, and only evil; those which do not admit of being changed into any thing good, but which require to be expunged altogether. Among these are those corrupt acquired instincts which have become the inheritance of fallen man, hatred, malice, revenge, deceit, cruelty, acquired lusts, and selfishness in its myriad forms. These, we have seen, when once acquired, are transmissive from one generation to another. They are not subject to the law of God, neither indeed can be, because in their essential character they are the very opposites of the Divine nature. They are that "body of death" which all along through the centuries has formed and stratified upon our burdened humanity, and which can in no wise be incorporated with it, but which must be rolled off, as the burden of the pilgrim rolled away when he came to the cross. Under the *second* division we place the natural appetites, affections, and powers; and these are good or evil according to their ultimate *ends*, according to the service in which they are used. Under the control of the Divine law they are good, under the control of the selfish nature they are evil. The appetites are good when they serve the higher nature; when their end is self-indulgence, they degenerate into brutal sensuality. Family affections are good and pure when their end is mutual improvement and aid; bad when their end is mutual indulgence and the exhibition of family pomp and pride. Nothing can be so disinterested as a mother's love. Nothing, again, can be so intensely and intolerably selfish. Family affections bring us into a more tender and loving fellowship with all the families of men, or else they are the forms of a noxious self-love, and they differ from those of a gross personal selfishness only because they reflect its hateful fires in a circle removed one degree further from us. Men will even commit greater wrongs to aggrandize their families than they would to aggrandize themselves. Intellect, when enlisted in the service of God and humanity, pouring light upon man's path to guide him to happiness and to heaven and lead on the groping nations to their millennial era, is a sublime and beneficent power. When enlisted in the service of wrong, having private honor and advantage for its end, and leading astray by cunning arts and glozing sophistries, it is the very attribute of archangel ruined. These natural powers, therefore, whether intellectual or affectional, are good or bad according to the motive force by which they are impelled and guided. Between God on the one hand, and self on the other, they hang and tremble; but it is the tendency of hereditary corruption to make them sway in the wrong direction with cumulative weight; to make the balance come down on the side of evil. But under the *third* division we place those sacred capacities which are the crowning glory of human nature, the capacity already described, of receiving the Divine Light and Life and making God operative in man. This capacity does not "tend to all evil," but to all good, since it is the ground of the regeneration of the individual and the progress of the race. It implies too the power of choice; choice between the agencies which we will suffer to shape our characters; choice between the influence that comes down to draw us into the heavens by its sweet persuasions, and the influence that comes up from below and seeks to draw us downward by its infernal sorceries, — that power of choice in which consists the moral agency of man.

Now if by the term *human nature* we mean to include the forces belonging to the first two divisions here named, and exclude the last, doubtless it is inclined to all evil, and averse to all good. Man shut in to himself would be abandoned to all depravity. There is hereditary corruption that sways him from behind, and then his natural powers and affections have lost that equipoise which they had in primitive man, and are deflected towards the service of the selfish nature. Appetite, natural affection, and the natural reason would all go over to the service of the evil powers, and toil in the bondage of sin. On their swift and downward course they would rush into the most frightful outbreaks of wickedness. But if by human nature we mean the sum total of all its capacities, and therefore its receptivity of the Divine force itself, — its capacities that open inward towards immensity and immortality, and of choosing the guidance of that power that shall bear it sun-ward like the eagle, — then we ought to abandon the word "total" in describing its depravity, as leading to confusion of thought and unnecessary misunderstandings. Even that theory of conversion which makes it instantaneous would logically presuppose an inborn capacity to be converted. We take it, that it does not quite mean to confound man with brutes and fiends, and that there is some reason in the nature of things why sovereign grace should select human beings for its objects rather than wolves and tigers. Even, then, if the Holy Spirit were not, as we contend, the divine fire that warms in our heart of hearts, and from the dawn of existence seeks to kindle within us all holy affections, — even if the orbit of our being lay through spaces of total blackness until some sudden light came blazing through it like a comet, — still we must be so organized as to be receptive of the light when it comes and be acted upon beneficently by the new power whenever it strikes us. We do not see, then, that our account of human nature differs from that of these theorists, when consistent with themselves, so much in regard to its real and intrinsic powers and propensities as in regard to the Divine plan of acting upon them. This difference, we will not disguise, is sufficiently wide, — the difference of supposing the child to be born into a state of the dreariest orphanage, to do nothing but sin up to the era of his conversion, and to be educated for repentance, and of supposing him at first the child of a Father whose claiming voice he ever hears, and whose spirit, unless rejected, ever shines within him "as glows the sunbeam in a drop of dew." It is the difference between a regeneration which may commence with the very dawn of being and prevent the leprosy from ever appearing in the voluntary life, and the regeneration that finds man full grown in evil, and lifts him out of the pool of sin, and attempts to bring him to life as you bring back life to the drowned, which must be done, if at all, with unutterable pangs.

Nor yet, again, is it to be disguised, that some of the old formulas and terminologies exclude from the original constitution of man any such forces and capacities as we have placed under our third division. They even take from him the power of choosing any thing but pollution, and the capacity itself of receiving the Holy Spirit is only the result of a new creation. Calvin says of infants, "Though they have not yet produced the fruit of their iniquity, yet they have the seed of sin within them ; even *their whole nature is* as it were *a seed of sin*, and therefore cannot but be odious and abominable to God." * But the old formulas themselves become flexile to the all-renovating Spirit that sweeps them through, and dry

---

* Institutes, Book II. Ch. 1, Sec 8.

bodies of divinity find a new life forming under the ribs of death. No matter whether the ancient symbols remain or not. Unless swept away by God's reviving breath, they will be warmed and bent by it, and we cannot keep out of them the plastic spirit which creates all things new. Those who thought they were ruling opinions with an iron rod find, to their surprise, that the rod, like Aaron's, has "budded" in their hands. We may even wake up some pleasant morning, and find that we have written out here a chapter in that progressive orthodoxy which has made its ancient symbols pliant to the shape of modern ideas. Whether so or not, God's truth is moving surely on to its triumphs. Those petrifactions called creeds, the cooling down of the religious sentiment into solid crust, cannot contain or shut in a still deeper religious sentiment that swells beneath. Even the creed-makers had thoughts and inspirations which could not be condensed into the formulas, for the Eternal Word shone through them as through all. Calvin himself, after having made out that infants are abominable to God, goes on afterwards to represent, with admirable inconsistency, that they are the objects of the Divine love;* for the central truth of the Gospel could not escape him, that God's love to the world even in its fallen state was the reason why he gave his only begotten Son to redeem and save it. And Augustine asserts the identical doctrine which in this chapter we have

* Institutes, Book II. Ch. 16, Sec. 1, 2.

aimed to develop: "Wherefore in a wonderful and divine manner he both hated us and loved us at the same time. He hated us as being different from what he had made us; but as our iniquity had not entirely destroyed *his work in us*, he could at the same time in every one of us hate what we had done, and *love what proceeded from himself.*"

PART III.

THE NEW MAN.

IF ANY MAN BE IN CHRIST, HE IS A NEW CREATION. — 2 Cor. v. 17.

"'T is a new life: thoughts move not as they did,
With slow, uncertain steps across my mind;
In thronging haste, fast pressing on, they bid
The portals open to the viewless Wind,
Which comes not save when in the dust is laid
The crown of pride that gilds each mortal brow,
And from before our vision melting fade
The heavens and earth, — their walls are falling now!
Fast sweeping on, each thought claims utterance strong,
Storm-lifted waves swift rushing to the shore;
On from the sea they send their shouts along,
Back from the cave-worn rocks their thunders roar, —
And I a child of God, by Christ made free,
Start from death's slumbers to eternity." — JONES VERY.

CHAPTER I.

REGENERATION.

"Most of us are fragments and divorces, the products of some former violence or convulsion, but such is not he [the new man], but rather a fair planet on which Eden continues. Things to us the most irreconcilable are his sweet harmonies. He is most wilful when he is doing God's will. His human reason is most independent when he is recipient of a divine revelation; his truth and God's belong all the more severely to each, because they are the other's. The efforts of his genius are his obedience to a divine commission. . . . . . Whatever he thinks is a thought enriched; whatever he does is a marriage deed. Thenceforth his doctrines embodied and illuminated are sights and sounds, — things seen and heard." — J. J. G. WILKINSON.

WE propose now to display, in as clear a light as we can, the nature of regeneration, and the means by which it is accomplished. We devote this chapter to the first of these topics, — Who and what is the new man?

We trust the preceding chapters have partly anticipated the answer, and rendered the path of our present inquiry open and clear. Regeneration implies three things: first, a cleansing away of all hereditary corruption; secondly, a restoration of the natural powers and affections to their appropriate service, or changing their inclination from self and making them incline to God; thirdly, receiving the divine life through those capacities that open upward towards God, and towards his angels. It is obvious, however, that the divine work is accomplished in an order exactly the reverse of the one now stated. For the first ground of our regeneration is the spiritual nature, the immanence of the Divine Spirit in the human soul. Its commencing dawn is the coming on of that light that visits our infant being, until God shines within like another sun, diffusing warmth and radiance through our whole nature, and drawing us towards himself in the bonds of an all-attractive love. Then God becomes the prevailing force within us, and he bends our natural powers towards himself, and draws them all into his service. Appetite, affection, intellect, active powers, all yield to him and serve him. The end of animal appetite is not animal pleasure, but manly development; the end of parental instinct is not its own indulgence, but the highest good of offspring; intellect serves God and not self, and genius no longer sings war-songs and bacchanals, but is the prophet of God's hidden truth, and lifts its hymn to his praise. The possessory instinct is guided to new ends, and property is acquired and held, not for self-aggrandizement, but for beneficent activity and useful living. All the instrumentalities of earth are converted into a means for the highest culture, and the highest culture is a solemn preparation to serve God and humanity. So the whole object of life is changed; and the natural powers, whose balance inclined towards the selfish nature, have that balance reversed and all the faculties bend towards God. Lastly, all hereditary evil is expelled, — that gang of lusts and passions, and the brood of lies which they engender, which require to be killed, since they cannot be converted; to be scourged out of the temple, since they cannot be made fit for its service. They are the native savages that must not be spared, but exterminated, when God's chosen ones come in to take possession. They are what Paul calls the "old man with its lusts," which is to be "put off," or which is to be "crucified" and "buried." These are opposed to the Divine nature; and as God comes within us with growing effulgence and power, they are driven out before him, — not without man's effort and coöperation. It is the denial of these evil tempers and instincts, that causes the struggle in his nature, and costs him painful vigils and conflicts, as if his soul were the battle-ground between the hosts of heaven and the hosts of hell. But victory succeeds to victory, and when the last foe is slain, he walks in the strength and peace of God, free and joyous as the angels.

This spiritual change, when all its inward processes are laid open and displayed, appears as the pilgrim's progress from the city of Destruction to the city of God. And here let us guard from error. No one is *regenerated* unless he comes to something more than "indulging a hope," or so long as the land of promise lies off in the distance, and is not a present possession and fruition. The new man is not one who has got some mystic title-deed to the heavenly country hereafter. He is the man whose foot already is planted on its ground, and who breathes its fragrance; into whose soul, that is, heaven has passed and is passing now. For the change of death is merely external; it only removes our fleshly coverings. It does not remove *us;* it only takes off a veil. The natural man, with his lusts and world-ward inclinations impelling him one way, and the divine force acting through him and impelling him another way, is swaying between heaven and hell. He chooses between these two forces, and says which shall draw him to itself. If he chooses wrong, his inmost mind passes from change downward to change, until it is moulded into the very image of hell, and is drawn by the most secret affinities to its abodes. Its spirit breathes upon him now; he suffers its pains, he keeps carnival with its horrid jubilees, its gates open on his soul, he descends through them and they shut over him, and death only comes to take the bandage from his eyes, that he may look round on his habitation and his home. If he chooses right, then his inmost mind changes the other way, drawn up among the saints and the seraphim; heaven draws around his spirit, and folds him in; he breathes its airs, he is filled with its harmonies; he hears in his own moral nature its chimes hardly mellowed by distance; he holds fellowship with its shining ones; and death by and by unclogs his senses, and gives to his open vision the land of peace. The great sentence, Come, ye blessed! and Go, ye cursed! is the everlasting law which is executing itself every day upon us, and while yet in the flesh we get wide asunder as the poles with the impassable gulf between. So, then, we say that regeneration is obtaining possession, for it is passing into the society of the redeemed, which on earth and in heaven make but one communion. And if any one should object, that it is not given to man here on the earth to pass into these high spiritual frames, or pitch his tent on this mountain of golden peace, we simply take issue upon the fact; for we know those and read of those who have the world under their feet, with whom the struggle is past and the victory won; and God's angels are with them as "a camp of fire around." Still, it is undoubtedly true, that the work of regeneration is not generally *consummated* here; and the present condition of the Church and society and educational systems suggests that we need not seek far to find the reasons. But we are here describing what regeneration is in its own nature, its processes, and its consummation.

Let us now seek for some of the *characteristics* of the regenerate state. And we premise, that the new man is indicated by the new motives whence all his actions flow. There are three classes of motives by which we are impelled to seek the paths of duty and obedience. These are fear, and hope, and love. When an impenitent man first wakes up to a sense of his danger, the first motive that impels him very often is *fear*, fear of the dismal results into which he knows he is plunging. He feels that nothing awaits him but trouble and unrest as he sinks away into darkness. He flies to religion as a refuge of safety. It may be that his heart opens up its mysteries into his consciousness, and its uncleanness lies exposed in the light that gleams from above. But his obedience at first is compelled and outward. At best, his joys and raptures come and go, and do not pass into permanent frames. The Adam of consciousness is not dead, but only sleepeth, and sometimes it wakes again with terrible energy, and prevails. Still, at times he has prelibations of the heavenly peace and foreshadowings of a better world. And here, it may be, through genuine self-consecration and reliance on the Divine promise, he begins to *hope* for heaven. But hope of reward, as such, is not a motive very much higher than the fear of punishment. It may be, and often is, based on delusions and fictions in theology, before there is any change in the inward man. Reformation is not regeneration, conformity is not worship, the wording and rewording of liturgies is not prayer, and hope of heaven is not the peace of its commencing dawn. Not until the Spirit abiding within has melted the soul beneath the glow of the Divine charms, not until the angel band of heavenly affections comes in, and the gang of selfish lusts goes out, do old things pass away and all things become new. Then begins the highest motive-power, which is *love;* for he that loveth is born of God and knoweth him. When our regeneration is consummated, love expels every other power, and reigns supreme and undivided. Now the soul hungers and thirsts after righteousness, as for daily bread and for living waters.

Now we obey the commandments because we love them, and it is our meat and drink to do the will of the Father. Fear is cast out; hope of reward has no place, for the Divine service is its own great reward, its own exceeding joy. Obedience is sweeter to the soul than light is to the eye, and sin, not in its consequences, but in its own essential nature, is more bitter than death, and more loathsome than the grave. Inclination becomes a safe and unerring guide; for to do right we have only to follow our impulses, and do what we love. We follow after duty with a passion and an appetite. We need not reason out what duty is, and get at our result through uncertain and labyrinthine windings. We have but to follow our desires, since we cannot desire what is wrong. The Holy Spirit, transfused through all our faculties and all our cleansed affections, becomes itself an instinct of our being, making the soul one flaming and undivided passion that urges on to its object, as unerring as the instinct that urges the bee to her cell. Affection and truth are one. That is to say, truth does not teach one thing, and affection crave another. Truth shows us the way we love, and we love the way it shows, and so affection and truth are one principle of action, even as the light and heat make one ray in the solar beams, which create their own paradise where they fall. Then ceases the conflict within. There is no clashing of interest with interest, no balancing of one inclination against another, for none other force acts within us than God's impelling love. There is no self-denial, because there is no self to be denied. That is crucified and slain. We pass into that high state of which we had dreamed, and for which we had sighed, when we do just what we please, and all that pleases us we may do; when we have no painful duties to perform, since duty is the glad motion, the spontaneous play, of all our faculties.

There is a floating philosophy which teaches that the impulses and intuitions of human nature are a sure guide, because they are the inspirations of God in humanity. But it does not recognize the distinction between humanity fallen and humanity renovated, and thus it is liable all the while to confound the corrupt instincts of the natural man with the clarified affections of the man created anew. It has no rule to distinguish hereditary proclivities to evil from the divine impulsions which move us after hereditary evil is extinguished. It makes that a rule of action for sinful man, which can be a safe one only for the redeemed. It has no analysis that searches us and cleaves the evil from the good, setting one over against the other and saying, *Avoid ye that*, and *Follow ye this.* And so it would put us on the fiery waves of corrupt desire, and let us float passively along to destruction, if only we drift past flowery banks and spicy groves before the rapids begin. It confounds human nature in its chaotic state with human nature distributed, after the spirit has brooded upon it and reduced all things to their class and order. It is by a higher and a self-revealing philosophy, that we come, through self-denial, to that state of unchartered freedom in which there is no self to be denied, where our six days of toil and struggle have ended, and we enter on our sweet Sabbath of repose.

The regenerate state, again, is characterized by a new kind of worship. God is revealed as never before, the light and the joy of our whole being. He sees nothing in us now that he does not love, for he sees his own work and he calls it good. He glows within us as our life and peace, even as the sun loves to look into the placid lake and make his image there. We pass into that state of prayer which cannot be translated into the clumsy vehicle of words; that still communion, to which a ritual is a clog and a burden; that devotion which knows of no declensions, since the sun that warms it never sets. Its worship is not the worship of those who meet to chafe each other's zeal that is flagging and growing cold, and who leap on the altar and cut themselves with knives, because the fire will not come down. It is love communing with love; the sons of God shouting for joy, their worship jubilant and spontaneous as the song of the summer bird on the airs of morning.

The regenerate state is characterized by more external changes. The world within flings its hues and colorings over the world without, and in some sort creates it anew. The natural powers and faculties, even to the natural body, our most external envelopment being brought into the service of the highest sentiments, conforming to the divine life within, and made pliant to its touch, are transfigured by it and reflect its glories. We have often seen how heavenly affections will create a new face under the ugliest features; how the members yielded to unrighteousness and made flexile to the deforming passions are moulded by them, till the whole man becomes the image of the sin he loves. So it is that the spiritual nature operates its changes outward and downward; that the Adam of consciousness holds us like clay in his hands, and makes our members the moulds of his dehumanizing lusts, while the Christ of consciousness changes us back into the figure of divine affections. The "old man with his lusts" therefore is put off, even to his literal embodyment, as the new man is formed beneath and claims to fill and shape our most outward being, when we seem changed, and,

> "As a troop of maskers when they put
> Their visors off, look other than before."

Even Nature herself becomes changed, for how varied does she appear to us, according to the eyes through which we look, and whether we see her work as a hard material fact, or the picture-language that shadows forth immortal things. The natural man sees this world only from the natural side. No light from the other side shows him the meaning in humble affairs, and the redolence that breathes out of them, and the divine airs enfolding every object. It is the difference between seeing this world only as a material structure, contrived for man's present gratification, and viewing it as the scene of his training for the skies; as exhibiting an exterior and perishing beauty, and as penetrated by an intelligence everywhere infused, that copies out the Everlasting Mind and opens everywhere a holy bible to human ken. Jonathan Edwards has alluded to this change in describing his religious experience: "My sense of divine things gradually increased, and became more and more lively, and had more of inward sweetness. The appearance of every thing was altered; there seemed to be, as it were, a calm sweet cast or appearance of divine glory in almost every thing. God's excellency, his wisdom, his purity and love, seemed to appear in the sun, moon, and stars, in the clouds and blue sky; in the grass, flowers, and trees; in the water and all nature." And one of yet clearer prophetic insight than that of Edwards describes the same thing as a sense sublime

> "Of something far more deeply interfused,
> Whose dwelling is the light of setting suns,
> And the round ocean, and the breathing air,
> And the blue sky, and in the mind of man, —
> A motion and a spirit that impels
> All thinking things, all objects of all thought,
> And rolls through all things."

Last of all, the regenerate state is characterized by a new morality. Works are filled and vitalized by that angelic benevolence which is not complete until clothed and ultimated in action. The works of the natural man are done for wages. The fear of hell scares him from wrong-doing, or the hope of heaven lures him to work in the master's vineyard and bear the heat and burden of the day. Hence there is so much of sighing and fainting under the weary load of present duty, among those who look away to some future heaven where there will be nothing to do but play on golden harps and sing pleasant songs. Hence the religious life and the practical, here on this earth, have been so riven asunder, religion retreating away into conference-rooms and prayer-meetings, and cathedrals on whose mystic silence no murmur breaks from without, while the field, the workshop, the mart, and the hustings are bereft of her presence and left dreary and profane. Even when their work is done from a religious sense of duty, it is not always true that religion is in the work. Perchance it only commands the work to be done. Not so when the regenerate life clothes itself in new moralities. Then works are to the soul what utterance is to genius, whose necessity is, I must speak or else I die; and whose glorious conceptions lie on the soul like a burden, and flood it with a beauty which it cannot bear, until those conceptions are born into the actual world, and embodied in the canvas, the marble, and the epic song. Then genius sees its heaven coming down to earth, and taking form in outward things, and it stands face to face with its own lovely creations. So it is with the man created anew in Christ Jesus and inspired with heavenly sentiments. His appropriate works are where these sentiments are embodied in loveliest forms, and his daily duties become the poesy of life, always inspired from above, always fragrant with the breath of praise. Ideas of goodness, beneficence, justice, and truth, always rolling in upon the soul when filled and warmed with the supremely good and fair, always seeking on earth their imbodiment and resting-place, leave us no peace unless we will give them shape in outward things, and carve the substance of this world into their own bright and heavenly image. And then we are blest, supremely blest, for our daily prayer has its daily fulfilment, that God's will be done, as in heaven, so also on the earth. We greatly mistake the essential wants of humanity, if we suppose that the same relation between our inmost life and our outermost practice will not subsist after we have done with time. And perchance, because in the spiritual world forms and substances are more yielding and passive to the plastic spirit within, the moralities of heaven shall be more redolent of its life, and its forms be sculptured into more perfect moulds of the everlasting Truth and Beauty. What higher bliss can we sigh for, than that our feet may move on this swift obedience through the unending ages, bringing the loftiest ideals into the lowest actualities, and making the harmonies between these two our working song?

There is one qualification which we ought to make. We have described the regenerate man as one in whom instinct and impulse are a safe and unerring guide, since the heart can crave nothing that is wrong. We ought, however, to allow, that until not only the individual is changed, but until the world around him is changed also, the best man will here find sometimes a conflict between his feelings and duties. In the punishment of crime, in the great battle with wrong, we may be called to sacrifice and suffering, and the performance of what are called painful duties. But even so the regenerate man is sustained and cheered, and triumphs over pain; and as fast as the world around him is changed and renovated, these painful duties diminish. They will cease entirely, when not only the breast of the individual, but the world that lies about him, shall become truly the mirror of the skies.

The sum of our doctrine, then, on this vitally important subject is this.

Regeneration, in its internal nature and process, includes three things: —

First, the receiving the divine life into our inmost being through those capacities that open inward towards God and the spirit-world,— the divine life imparted by the Holy Spirit that ever breathes through the heart of humanity.

Secondly, moved by this divine and attractive force, our natural powers, intellectual, affectional, and active, incline towards God, and are drawn into his service.

Thirdly, all corrupt instincts, whether we acquired them ourselves or received them as the foul inheritance of the past, constituting the Adam of consciousness, are expelled. This is the old man which is put off as the new man is unfolded from within.

The new man is known and characterized, —

By the new motives which are the springs of conduct. Hope of reward and fear of punishment both give place to an ever-abounding love. In other words, we act not from motives drawn from the future, but from the glad promptings of the present hour. Hence, again, —

By a new kind of worship; for we do not seek God to purchase his future favor, or to deprecate his wrath, but because he is our present life and joy, and our powers lift the spontaneous hymn to his praise.

By a new enjoyment of external things, since the light and peace within us invest the world without us with their sun-bright hues, and since even the body which we wear is pliant to the new power that shapes the internal man, and makes the external reflect its radiance.

By the new morality in which the new life seeks expression and embodiment, when the soul puts on righteousness, and it clothes her, and makes justice her robe and diadem.

The means by which this great change is effected are as various as the culture and discipline of life. In the following chapters we shall attempt to group together those which seem of the most importance, and which often lie nearest at hand when we seek them not.

CHAPTER II.

CHOICE.

"How precious a thing is youthful energy! if only it could be preserved, entirely *englobed* as it were within the bosom of the young adventurer, till he can come forth and offer it a sacred emanation in yonder temple of truth and virtue! But alas! all along, as he goes towards it, he advances through an avenue formed by a long line of tempters and demons on each side, all prompt to touch him with their conductors and draw the divine electric current with which he is charged away." — JOHN FOSTER.

No diligent and candid reader of the Sacred Scriptures can fail to have discovered that the spirit-world is described by them under two classes of images. They open above us a region of infinite purity and love, where all that is good and happy is parted off by itself, and hangs above us like a firmament of grandeur and beauty. They open beneath us a region where sin in its hideous shape sinks away to its own level, and seeks the hiding-places of a starless night. These two states are set over one against the other. It is the parallelism that runs through the whole Bible, and you scarcely open a page where you do not trace its lines distinctly and sharply drawn. No middle region is described in the land of souls. And this world of sense and matter is spoken of as hanging midway between those two great kingdoms of Light and of Shadow. The world we now live in, mixed up as it is of good and evil, is constantly yielding back its primal elements, decomposing and parting off, on the one hand, the worthless dross, and, on the other, the clear and imperishable gold. Good and evil dissolve and part off by themselves, the good rising by its own affinities and seeking its kindred heaven, thus pouring ever fresh streams of life and blessedness into its abodes. The bad parts away, and is drawn to its like in the abysses, because there too is its kindred and its home.

This doctrine we find drawn out in the parable of the tares and the wheat, growing together until the harvest, when the former are gathered into bundles and piled up for burning, and the latter is stored away in its garners. We find it touched off with a most graphic pencil in the parable of the sheep and the goats, where the Son of man sits among the assembled nations, and, as the solemn drama passes along, they part asunder under the opposite sentences, Come, ye blessed! and Depart, ye cursed! We find it, again, in the parable of the rich man and Lazarus, symbolized in the great gulf that lies between the realm of Light and Bliss, and the realm of Shadow and Pain. And again we find it in the Apocalypse, where the new heaven shines above, beautiful as a bride, and the lake of fire lies beneath, with all unclean things that float on its noxious waves. And yet again we find it in our Saviour's description of a twofold resurrection; of those who have done good coming out of their graves to higher life and fruition, and of those that have done evil to a resurrection of condemnation and shame.

Now it is somewhat surprising, at first thought, that, while the Scriptures abound in all this moral painting, it should have no greater power over the consciences and lives of men; that, while these pictures are hung down out of the spirit-world into this, they have failed so much in arresting the gaze of mortals. We read over some tragedy that paints the happiness or the sufferings of human beings, and we thrill and weep at the winding up of its scenes. We take up some story of human fortunes abounding in human loves and interests, and we hang breathless over its catastrophes. Why is it, then, that the solemn drama of humanity, and the winding up of its fortunes, do not take hold of our deepest sympathies?

We apprehend the reason to be, that to many, perhaps to most minds, there is, after all, an appearance of unreality in these descriptions; that they do not seem to have any basis in known facts, or to paint human character as we know it and see it. Perhaps an objection may lie in the mind of the reader somewhat after this wise.

We do not see any such division of human character as answers to these pictures and images. Men are not all good, nor all bad, but between the best man and the worst there is every shade of character, where the colors run into each other. Take the highest grade of excellence that was ever attained to, take the lowest point of depravity to which humanity has ever fallen, and where on this descending scale will you put your finger and make a dividing mark, and say that all above are bound to one destiny and all below to another? The man just above it differs only in the slightest shade from the man just below it. Good and evil are mixed up in every man's soul. They change and interpenetrate in all imaginable shapes and colorings. This division line, therefore, is merely arbitrary, and so a just and holy being can never make it.

Now we hold and acknowledge that the facts of this life present a perfectly fair and valid ground from which to argue the facts of the life to come. Away, we say, with all theologies which sunder themselves from human nature. Man, as an immortal being, has only one continuous and endless life. It is not a life to be chopped into fragments which have no relation to each other. The future is an unfailing result of the present. The spirit-world is human nature more fully revealed and its powers more perfectly dramatized, and unless the ground of this picture-language of the Bible exist now and here in these throbbing bosoms, it exists never and nowhere.

But let us be cautious, and not reason from appearances only. And we go on to show that the objection, which we have endeavored to draw out in its full strength, is specious and delusive. It is founded, we think, on shallow views of human nature, not on a perception of its more deep and intense realities.

For consider the matter. Is it not true that every man who comes to years of moral choice and responsibility has some purpose that governs him and gives unity to his life? Analyze your motives and you will find it so. Every heart has its ruling passion, every life has its ruling principle. It is true that, under the urbanities and simulations of life, this does not always appear. But could you lay off from any one's heart all its envelopments till you came to the real man, you would find some principle to which all others held a secondary and subordinate place. From the very constitution of human nature it cannot be otherwise. Human nature opens outward towards sense and inward towards God. The forces of hereditary corruption assail it from behind, and would draw it into the bondage of self and the world, while divine forces act upon it from within and above, and would draw it into the service of God and humanity. We must choose between these two. On every human being devolves the fearful responsibility of being arbiter between them, and deciding which of these forces shall prevail. There, on his right hand, comes down the angel of truth, unrolling before him the Divine commandments, and pointing with directing finger to the bright and climbing pathway. There, on his left hand, stands at the same time the fiend of self, with his glozing seductions and lies. Is there any man to whom the angel of God's presence hath not come bringing the Everlasting Law, whether in the revelations of Christianity or in those veiled interior ministries which wait on the human soul under every form of religion and worship? And is there any one whom the tempter hath not approached on the side of the selfish nature, that he might warm into life all the germs of hereditary evil, and make that the dominant power of the soul? And doth it not appear, then, even as the Scriptures have put the alternative, that no man can serve two masters, since, while he follows and loves the one, he rejects and denies the other? He chooses between them. And they are opposites. They have nothing in common. One begets in us the faith and the affections, the graces and virtues, which belong to the regions of light; the other, those delusions and passions and corroding memories that people the realm of shades.

But perhaps the reader will object, and say, "You do not yet meet the case. What if every man has his ruling principle, a principle chosen, if you will, from the code of heaven or of hell? The best man does not live up to his own ideal, and is not all a saint. He has his faults and his short-comings. So the worst man is not all self. He has his virtues and his better feelings, and his character is not all dark and ugly." This is all true. But then it is also true, that the wrong principle, once chosen and followed and made vital, becomes central and controlling, and the virtues and graces are driven out towards the surface of the man. Such a man will do many good things, when they are not inconsistent with his main object and aim. He may even make the virtues his auxiliaries, and they shall subserve his purposes. But when the selfish nature and the Eternal Law come fairly and directly in conflict, one must yield, and in this case it is uniformly the latter, while the other becomes ascendant. And so the wrong principle encroaches upon all his powers, and has dominion over his whole nature. His character does not yet lie in total eclipse. But the line which separates the light and shade is moving the wrong way; and how long will it be, unless he changes and makes a new choice and so reverses the process, before that which should have been the guide of his life hangs darkling in the sky? The dominant principle, the ruling love, shape the character more and more into their own resemblance and effigy, till even the virtues and graces are only hollow expediencies and imitations, — outside decorations, like flowers that blossom upon graves.

And so, on the other hand, though every good man falls short of his standard, yet if he follows it in good faith, it leads him higher and higher. The selfish nature is denied, till finally it ceases to be. Selfish principles and passions hold a subordinate place. They are driven from the centre to the surface. The line of shade recedes, till the light of his life emerges clear and full in the heavens. Whoever, in short, chooses the right, and is ruled by it, grows better and better. Whoever chooses the wrong, and is ruled by that, grows worse and worse. Is not this human nature? It is true that this process working within us in the very core of our being does not always appear at once upon the surface. But the man whose principle of life is wrong has his internal character constantly transforming into the false and the evil. And this may go on awhile under a fair exterior, under the show of morality, under the show of worship itself. But all these externals are to fall away. We rise into the spirit-world with no disguises about us, where the inner life is brought forth in open and substantial manifestation.

To our apprehension, therefore, this moral painting of the Bible, which parts men off into opposite groups and companies, becomes most intensely real. The deep-working principles of human nature are prophetic of this grand consummation, and make these results inevitable. We may choose which class of forces shall sway us. But having chosen, our souls are moved on by impulsions which we cannot reverse or divert from their crisis. If no Bible had opened to us a revelation of things to be, human nature were itself a Bible whose open pages would disclose this final catastrophe.

We ought, however, to concede so far to the objection which we have in hand, as to allow that self-love takes various forms, from the most malignant to the most mild, and that the great principle which, with unerring precision, cleaves asunder the good and the evil, does not separate the one into the same state of fruition, nor part off the other into one mass of woe. Neither heaven nor hell is one, but multiform, and the law of a just retribution will be applied to us, when we shall reap down the harvest which we sow. What we argue is, that God and self, good and evil, heaven and hell, are opposite in nature and principle, and by no skill of the pencil can one be made to shade off into the other. By no contrivance, divine or human, can they be made to dwell together in peace, but they tend to separation by their own elective affinities, and their struggles towards that separation occasion the perturbations of this our state of mingled good and evil. The good angel stands on one side, and the evil genius on the other. We hear the first in a thousand pleadings and calls to duty. We hear the other in the seductions of self-interest and self-indulgence. We follow one or the other, and so our most internal character is changing from glory to glory, or from shade to deeper shade. This power of choice, then, is an awful power. The child, as soon as he can understand the words Right and Wrong, stands between the world of Light and the world of Shadows. He comes into society. Two rules of action are placed before him, that of the Gospel and that of the world. He chooses between them. He makes one supreme and subordinates the other, for there is no middle ground. If he chooses the first, the good angel ever beckons him on in a path that finally opens upward into fields of everlasting fruition. If he chooses the other, the path leads downward,—how easy at first to tread! but it grows darker and more rugged, till his feet stumble on the dark mountains, and he falls benighted into the abyss below.

The test here presented, we say, is philosophical, and stands clear of the cabbalistic theologies.

There is no long and crabbed creed to be learned, no mystic experience to be had through charms and conjurations, no faith in mere dogmas to be "imputed for righteousness." Turn where you will, reader, there are two principles of conduct written out and blazing upon you, one of self and one of Christ. On the one hand is the Gospel, and on the other are the world's hollow maxims and shifting expediencies. As soon as you rise in the morning, the right and the wrong present their alternatives in every deed you do. No subtile system of ethics needs unfolding. There is the path on the right, and there on the left. Under one of two ruling motives, every deed ranges itself at once. And though the divergence between these two paths may seem at first slight and unimportant, yet that is the starting-point of all the differences that follow after. They have been compared to two lines starting from the same point. However small the angle they make, they diverge wider and wider the farther they extend. And if infinitely extended, they diverge to an infinite distance. So between two persons choosing, one a right rule of life, and the other the wrong. Their characters at first may not seem so very different, but the fatal angle is there!

So much depends on this fearful power of choice, the first power to be exercised when our regeneration begins. On these silent volitions of the breast hang such amazing and eternal fortunes. No wonder, then, that such powers wait upon us, to bend our will upward or deflect it downward. And no wonder that, to impress upon us the importance and consequences of moral choice, God has hung down to us out of eternity the roll of destiny, painting on one of its folds the upper world, with its hills and vales reposing in the soft beams of peace, and on the other, that world over which roll the clouds of an unavailing sorrow, — yet clouds which conceal far more than they disclose!

An Eastern monarch, on the eve of battle, stood surveying the countless battalia that swarmed in the plain beneath him, till he burst into a flood of tears. "Why do you weep," said his courtiers, "for the victory will soon be ours." "I weep," said he, "to think that in one hundred years not one of these hostile myriads will be alive." But the Christian imagination forms to itself a conception more august and solemn. The myriads that swarm over the earth's surface! To-day alive and busy; to-morrow brushes them from the scene. And amidst infinite varieties of taste, affection, and motive, two master motives are severally supreme. Every heart has been touched and polarized by one of two opposite magnets: death comes to remove outward and artificial restraints, and lo! this mass of humanity separates and sweeps towards its opposite poles.

If, when these momentous alternatives were first presented, — for they *are* presented to every human being, — if, when first he heard the pleadings of the angel in his breast, or the sorceries of the tempting fiend, this power of choice were exercised with decision on the side of right, and the life of regeneration chosen with alacrity and energy, all else would follow in its time and order. This vow once made, and this great work of self-consecration once commenced in good faith, we have the promise that more agencies than we can take notice of wait upon us, that they may smooth out our way before us. This efficient exercise of the power of choice, — choice between the motive-powers that shall rule us, choice between the two worlds that draw us contra-wise, and fling over us the alternations of sun and shade, — is the first step in the Christian life, and that step firmly taken, the victory is half won. For the heavens themselves then bend around us to guard us on, and our decision, we are assured, sends through their ranks a wavelet of joy.

CHAPTER III.

THE BOOKS OPENED.

"I presuppose a humble and docile state of mind, and above all the practice of prayer as the necessary condition of such a state, and the best, if not the only, means of becoming sincere to our own hearts; — those inward means of grace, without which the language of the Scriptures, in the most faithful translation, and in the purest and plainest English, must nevertheless continue to be a dead language, — a sun-dial by moonlight." — COLERIDGE.

It is an obvious condition of man's regeneration, that he know himself. He must see the evil that is in him, in order to its extrusion. And yet so manifold are the envelopments that infold him, that he bears about unscanned the mysteries that lie within. We live mainly in externals, and hence we are disguised from ourselves. Hence our imperfect view of human nature; hence our shallow culture, — so often the outside gilding that conceals a heart uncleansed; hence our surface-moralities; hence our ignorance of the deepest springs of action in our own bosoms. What is inly wrong, in order to be apprehended and expelled, must come within the clear range of our inward vision. How shall we have these self-revealings? By what means is the book of our life to be opened?

There is a way which is simple and direct, to him

who earnestly desires to see himself as he is. It is by turning the soul towards God. It is by communing with the Eternal Purity, whose spirit ever broods over the chaos within us, and seeks to separate its elements into determinate form and order. Before the Divine nature, all that is wrong in our own is revealed by contrast, and appears black in the light. The Eternal Law shines down through our being, and shows our desires and aims, in opposition to its own sanctity. It is the hatefulness of the selfish will in the presence of the All-Pure. Doubtless, the revelation is at first humiliating and painful. In that hour of self-conviction, the burden of our most inherent corruption hangs heavy on our souls. Two ideas, for the time, take sole possession of our minds, and fill the whole scope of our vision. Our inmost self how alienated! The Divine nature how dazzling and dreadful in its holiness! The contrast between these two makes us veil our faces in tears, and exclaim, "I shall die, for I have seen the Lord!" We cannot bear that "noon of living rays," when searched and laid open beneath it. He who thought himself rich and in need of nothing, now finds himself poor and in need of every thing. He who before was complacent and satisfied with the shows of a seeming morality, is startled and dismayed, as a light from out of himself is let down through the central places of his being, and reveals the secret corruption that lurks through all its winding recesses. How false has been his standard of right, how low have been his aims, and what impurities have tainted the springs of his conduct! "I thought myself alive without the law," said the great Apostle, "but when the commandment came, sin revived, and I died." When the Eternal Law shone forth, the sin that was in me came full into the range of my consciousness, and instead of spiritual life, I found there a mass of death. Thus God, by his immanence in man, reveals, when invoked and welcomed, the afflicting contrast between human corruption and the Everlasting Purity.

What we have now described, is sometimes called "conviction of sin." But it is more than that. Sin pertains only to what is wrong in our volitions and actions. But now the sources of sin, lying deeper than all volition and action, are shown to us; for the vain disguises of our self-love having withered away under the beams of the Divine countenance, the diseased mass whose hidden motions had swayed our volitions and conduct is disclosed, and makes us cry, "Who shall deliver us from this body of death?" The Apostle, as above quoted, is not using the words *sin* and *death* as the synonyma of moral guilt, but rather of moral disease, from which guilty conduct flows as from a turbid spring. How often had our endeavors after holiness been defeated and baffled! how had the means of grace been repeated till they had become state formalities! how had our vague dissatisfactions and our daily unrest prevented the peace of God and our sweet repose on the bosom of his love! The source of all our trouble has now been shown to us, as a new page in the book of our life has opened to our sight.

CHAPTER IV.

THE BOOKS OPENED.

"O, what a sight were man, if his attires
Did alter with his mind,
And, like a dolphin's skin, his clothes combined
With his desires!

"Surely, if each one saw another's heart,
There would be no commerce,
No sale or bargain pass: all would disperse
And live apart!

"Lord, mend, or rather make us; *one* creation
Will not suffice our turn:
Except thou make us daily, we shall spurn
Our own salvation." — George Herbert.

There is a legend of one of the ancient kings of England, that, returning from the Crusades, he was taken captive by his enemies, and confined in a German fortress. Languishing there in the darkness of his solitary cell, he was lost to his people and dead to the world, and fast perishing from the memory of mankind. But there was a minstrel of his court by the name of Blondel, who sought to find him. He wandered in disguise through Europe, and played and sung under the windows of every prison, the airs which he and his master had sung together in days of old. At the last trial, after the first strain had died away, the second strain awoke from within the fortress, and rolled responsive from the prison cells. The lost monarch was found.

Precisely such is the office which temptation performs for us. It reveals us. We mean by temptation, such surroundings as make us conscious of wrong desires, and draw us vehemently towards forbidden objects. Any one seeking in good faith to know himself, may find all the shadings of his inmost being reflected back upon him, from the objects that lie along his path. For temptation puts nothing new into us. It only brings out before the sun something which existed there already. We are enticed by the lusts that are within, and it is the lust which gives to the object without all its meretricious and seducing charms. The corruption within corresponds to the object without, and they call and answer to each other. If there were no lurking evil in our nature, there could be no temptations. They are the Blondels, whose songs and harpings are of the same air and dialect of some corruption within ; and so they respond to each other, strain for strain. Hence there is a meaning in the discipline of life, the myriad-toned language that comes to us from without, which we do not always seek to comprehend. One of the first designs of Providence in leading us through the paths of our probation here, is to show us to ourselves. The guilty man says, in extenuation of his crime, "If I had not been sorely tempted, I should not have fallen." So neither would you have known the evil that is in you. Providence led you into the midst of these surroundings, for the purpose, not of causing you to sin, but of showing you your propensities to sin, as if he had said, "Behold, I show you a mystery!" How often has a man thought himself immaculate, until the attractive power of some object out of him caused the lurking corruption to leap up in his bosom. So it is with all the passions that lie coiled within. Circumstances do not create them; they only evoke them from their mystic places into the light of our self-consciousness. One person brings into the world a revengeful temper. But who knew it while the infant was smiling in the cradle? It is along with the provocatives of opposition, that it discovers its full strength and malignity. Another inherits a selfish love for acquisition. But it is not the infant brow that is pursed with calculation. It is amid competitions and scrambles for gain, it is among lands and stocks and treasures, that he feels the gnawings of the accursed hunger for gold. The lust for place and power does not point to its unscrupulous arts, and the depths of its cringing baseness, until occasion and circumstance have uncoiled it, and we see its amazing possibilities. Thus are we led along the paths where the objects of our selfish love stir up the passions of the heart; and then, if we will but watch its motions, we shall find those passions unwinding, one after another, until our inward life has been imaged back upon us, — and then we have seen ourselves! All the corruption of our natures asserts its existence. We may deny it, we may slay it now if we will, and it shall never pass into our voluntary life. But in all its shapes it shall thus pass before the eye of self-consciousness, as clearly as the forms of future dynasties passed before the wizard-glass of Banquo.

It often occurs, that those who have never had these self-revealings will contemplate their own deeds with the deepest amazement. Their passions lay still within them like caged and sleeping lions, and they might have been led along under a dispensation of terror that overwhelmed and repressed their free moral agency, and their outward lives would have been perfectly blameless. But rather than human nature should bear onward all this hidden defilement, Providence permits these secret forces to be uncaged and set free; and so they who will not seek a knowledge of themselves by self-examination and prayer are suffered to obtain it at the cost of bitter repentance and blasting remorse. "Is thy servant a dog, that he should do this great thing?" Who is Hazael, the blameless Syrian, that he should be thought capable of such awful crimes? And the prophet answered, "The Lord hath shown me that thou shalt be king over Syria."

Even the crimes of society, the collective man, might reflect back upon the individual the lurid colors of his own passions. Whence come wars and fightings? They are the ultimation of the lusts of every man who loves not his neighbor as himself. Our selfish instincts are cruel as the grave. Hatred, love of rule, and the greed for gain, first rankle in the individual breast; they poison domestic and social relations, they demoralize parties, and finally they set nation against nation, and then they are in full blaze, giving the world an open view of the hell that had glared beneath. They are precisely the same lusts which, in private life, make man unjust or unkind to his brother, — only now they have obtained volume, and passed into combustion by union and contact; and it is amid the demon-cries of the battle-field, where the collective man is in action, that a permissive Providence confronts an unregenerate human nature with its own ghastly image.

If some being were to alight upon this earth, his spirit susceptible only of those desires that glow in the seraph's frame, he would walk through all its corruptions with no thirst for its sinful pleasures. Yet the same environments that evoke from the unregenerate heart its unhallowed desires, only set free the angel's affections and sympathies when that heart is purified of evil. Opposition calls forth from the natural man wrong for wrong. From the breast of the Divine Man, a flood of heavenly tenderness was set free by the hand that smote it. Our regeneration, therefore, is consummated, not when we resist temptation merely, but when temptation is impossible, and no Blondel's harp can wake an echo to its strain.

There is another province of human probation, similar to the one just described, which is called *trial.* It is trial in the strictest sense of the word, for it is the grand assay which distinguishes the worthless dross from the pure gold. The first effect of suffering and affliction is to test man and to reveal him. It were easy to keep him in the way of obedience, by the pressure of outward motives. He puts on the blandishments and urbanities of the world, and every appetite is pampered, while the world calls him good and generous. He puts on the shows and seemings of worship, and he easily persuades himself that its sanctities enter into him in proportion to the solemnity and splendor of its ceremonials. Perhaps the deceiver has no art so cunning, and so often practised, as that which imposes upon a man by taking from him the substance of religion, and giving him its painted shell. He violates none of the moralities, he reads his Bible, he cons his liturgies and his prayers, and under a thin crust of respectability he conceals himself from himself, and perhaps from his fellow-beings, because he does no wrong. Why should he do wrong, when the pressure from without keeps him perforce in the right? But strip him of these adventitious circumstances, take off the outward pressure, and let the inner man of the heart be released. Then it is often found that change of scene changes apparently the whole character, while really it has only disclosed it by taking off the shams that invested it.

Both sacred and profane historians describe the scene within the walls of Jerusalem during its siege by the Roman army. The daughters of Judah late-ly walked her streets in glory and pride. They "make a tinkling with their footclasps, mincing their steps as they go." But now famine rages, and conventional rules are snapped asunder like threads. See the relative strength of the benevolent and selfish feelings, while hunger and despair rend away their disguises, and set them free. Where now is religion, that came with votive offerings to the temple? where maternal love, of late clinging so fondly to her babes? "The tender and delicate woman that would not adventure to set the sole of her foot upon the ground for delicateness and tenderness, her eye is evil toward her son and toward her daughter and toward her little one, for *she killed and ate them* for want of all things, secretly, in the siege." Even such are the susceptibilities and fountains in the heart which may be hidden under a glare of grandeur. And so, betimes, the Divine Providence uncovers this under-world of passion and motive, and brings all its secrets into day.

Hence come our trials, not often with crushing weight, but with such sharp severity as to cleave into our hearts and open them to our gaze. God smites our idols, that he may measure to us the extent of our idolatry. Not until then did we know whether this world or the other was supreme in our affections. Not until then did we know whether we had any faith or not. We are living in conformity with Christian rituals, and think we believe in immortality. Perhaps, in some such hour of self-confidence, "we have all been touched and found base metal." The death-angel comes near us; our loved ones fall around us, they seem to drop into blank nothingness, and we see then how earthly prospects had shut out the heavens, how infidel are our griefs, and how selfish our fondest loves. Or perhaps, broken by sickness, and wrung with chronic pains, the sufferer foregoes the prospects and pleasures which mankind so highly prize. We wonder what all this means, till presently we see the meekest piety and the most deep and untroubled devotion evolved from this very condition; and when Resignation there appears leaning on her lowly and beautiful altar, and faith rises triumphant over pain, we are ready to pray for the same sharp instrumentalities, if so be they may work out for us the same exceeding weight of glory. For first they cleave into our natures and lay them open, albeit we lie lowly and bleeding, and then we know our deeper wants, and what we should seek, and what we should mortify and deny.

We have heard much, and not unprofitably, of the dangerous tendencies of lax systems of religion and morals. Perhaps it does not occur to every one, that a religion of artificial austerity and gloom, though less dangerous to the state, brings a more deadly peril to the individual. It keeps the outward man from sinning, without cleansing the man within. It does not remove the depravity out of man, but drives it in towards the centre of his being, — out of his own sight perhaps, — and fixes and congeals it there. He walks the path of obedience with trembling step, his soul never swept with the gales of Divine Love. But in another world, if not in this, the inner man must come forth and meet its own dismal retributions. These artificial motives cease to act, our sham-work falls away from us, and the natural heart appears just as it is, and fills its sphere of life with its own hideous shapings and colorings. And yet many a timid believer has been driven into some grim-looking "ark of safety," to escape from the fire-storms which were expected to come down upon all who remained outside. They are safe from the storms without, but not from the pent-up magazines within. That religion is the most safe, and that discipline the most merciful, which explores the heart most thoroughly, and pours the noontide into its chambers.

Have you, reader, ever experienced a great sorrow? and if so, have you not seen afterwards how it discloses heights and depths in your spiritual nature which you had never known, and resources upon which you had never drawn; how it produces susceptibilities which you had never before felt; how it induces a tenderness of mind that makes it ductile almost as the clay, and ready to receive the stamp of the Divine image; how little animosities and hatreds are banished and forgotten, while the heart has new yearnings towards all that live, and especially towards all that suffer; how the soul sickens at mere shows and appearances, and demands realities, while it hungers after the good and the true; how this world recedes and grows less, while the world of immortality comes on as if now first revealed, and incloses you in its light,—just as, when the glare of the day is withdrawn, and the darkness moves over us, we gaze on a new sky, and bathe in the starry splendors of the Milky Way?

CHAPTER V.

THE BOOKS OPENED.

"There was silence, and I heard a voice."—Job iv. 16.

PERHAPS we are as little given to meditation and solitude as any people on the face of the earth. And yet among the most important aids to self-knowledge are the holy ministries of silence; and there cannot be self-inspection at all without it. People must have, they think, one of three things, books, company, or business, else time is lost and the hours drag heavily along. Their minds must be taken up with other people's thoughts, with the clatter of words, or with the plunge into affairs. Even religious exercises, as they are often conducted, tend more to hide the individual heart than to reveal it. The world is full of noise, and there is as much noise about religion as about business, and sometimes a great deal more. When one is always seeking to get a quantity of emotion poured into him, that he may pour it out again, or to have his heart-strings played upon among sympathizing crowds, he will often think he has "got religion," till in some hour of solitary temptation or midnight silence he finds his true self had been lost sight of, and that in the midst of numbers he had failed to hear the most internal beatings of his own heart.

Has the question never pressed painfully upon the reader, What manner of person shall I find myself when death has torn away all the concealments of sensible things and I stand alone with God? What might I see if my heart of hearts were to symbolize itself before me, and I saw all its secrets standing out like pictures on the wall? Paul even had revolved this question anxiously, lest, having preached unto others, he himself should be cast away. We have the means of obtaining answers to these questions which shall not be altogether indistinct.

We shall find, by a little experiment and analysis, that the thoughts, images, and feelings that we have, come from two very different sources. First, they are suggested or forced upon us from without. They are poured in upon us from natural objects, from engrossing affairs, from converse with books and men. None of *these* trains of thought and feeling are strictly and entirely ours. They were put into us; and it may be that they have overlaid and concealed our deeper affections and sentiments. But there is another source of thought and imagery, and that is, *our hearts in their spontaneous workings*. When these thoughts and images come solely from within, when there is no sound and no object to suggest them and they arise of themselves and come up throng after throng through the brain, we may know that they originate in the life-cells of our being, and that they wear the colors of our own affections. We never know so well what is in us as in such moods as these. In order to this, all external things must be shut out from the sight and all sounds must die upon the ear. For this very purpose Providence has arranged the economy of our affairs, that the noise and the silence shall alternate each with the other, for at the close of every day he arrests the busy throng and hangs around the curtains of darkness, and there is no voice in the streets and no sound of wheels and footsteps; —

> "When fades the glimmering landscape on the sight,
> And all the air a solemn stillness holds."

Would we know, therefore, whether the heart be clean within, and how it would be likely to appear when these outward swathings have been stripped from us and its hidden processes lie exposed? In an hour when the wings of silence are brooding upon the spirit, and all external scenery has been blotted out, watch the thoughts and fancies that come up from within! Be simply a spectator; let them come of themselves, and sweep away as they will. Then it might often be found, that he who thought himself regenerate would discover impure fountains in his heart; would see evil thoughts and corrupt imagery coming up out of it and thronging the chambers of the brain; would see memories coming back from places of forbidden pleasure, and looking pleasant as in days of old; would find that sin had its charms and lures, and that he rolled it as a sweet morsel under his tongue, — that the whole style of his thoughts was earthly and not heavenly, selfish and sensual, and not spiritual and pure.

I would not even lose the benefit of the dreams that visit my pillow, of which Charles Lamb said, more truly perhaps than he intended, "We try to spell in them the alphabet of the invisible world, and think we know already how it shall be with us." For what are they, and what do they mean? They are the motions of our involuntary machinery. By our voluntary powers we array about us such scenery as we will, and sit down amid sights and sounds that please and regale the senses. But when the voluntary powers are suspended, the involuntary are wide awake, and they paint a new scenery about us: they dip their pencils in our most secret desires, and in the colors of those desires they set all things in array about us. They are the Guidos and Raphaels of our inner world, and their shadings and colorings are often the true representations of the inner life. A man shall then find, perhaps, his most cherished plans and most secret inclinations out of him. He shall see his secret self projected in the images that float around, and form the skies and landscapes of this microcosmic and spirit realm, suggesting to us that sure and deep-working spiritual law by which the celestial and infernal scenery are produced, — the heaven and hell hereafter, which are the *exfigurations* of a redeemed or a lost humanity. If therefore the objects of pursuit which these involuntary powers array before us are mainly wrong, and the scenery which they paint is prevailingly impure, we may know that we need cleansing yet; for when our physical and spiritual natures are both brought into entire harmony with Divine laws, their involuntary motions even shall produce no images but those of white-robed innocence.

But there is another privilege which comes from the holy ministries of solitude and silence. It is solemn, devout, intense meditation. There is comparatively little of this. There is much reading and meeting-going, and hurrying to and fro on business, but little of the brooding spirit of thought. And yet without the latter there is hardly such a thing as thorough self-knowledge and repentance. Men are moved in masses, or trained to the observance of conventional rules, and think themselves tolerably good. But not till they get out of the crowd and go away, alone, and there study the Divine law, and apply it to their individual failings and proclivities, does the secret heart lie exposed, and the light of self-conviction flash down through all its windings, and the beauteous light break on them from afar for whose repose they inly sigh. We live in external things and seek external excitements. And thus the mind takes into itself so much of what is coarse and earthly. Modern Christendom has abundance of Pharisees and Sadducees, and formalism and sensualism are not likely soon to pass away. But where are its Essenes, who sit alone in the solemn shadows where contemplation explores the starry deeps? We need to pass alternately from the inward to the outward, and from the outward back again to the inward; for unless we seek these meditative moods, we sink lower and lower, till we are buried in sense. We lose all heavenly-mindedness, all clear intuition. We lose the tidings of immortality that float around us, and sound fainter and fainter within us. We lose that knowledge of ourselves which is the first condition of our regeneration, and without which all other knowledge is superficial. And we never ascend the glory-smitten summits whence a contemplative faith gazes full into the opening Paradise of God.

CHAPTER VI.

ANOTHER BOOK OPENED.

"The mind of man desireth evermore to know the truth according to the most infallible certainty which the nature of things can yield. The greatest assurance generally with all men, is that which we have by plain aspect and intuitive beholding. Where we cannot attain unto this, there what appeareth to be true, by strong and invincible demonstration, such as wherein it is not in any way possible to be deceived, thereunto the mind doth necessarily assent, neither is it in the choice thereof to do otherwise. And in case these both do fail, then which way greatest probability leadeth, thither the mind doth evermore incline." — HOOKER, ECC. POLITY, II. 7.

THERE are, we premise, two kinds of revelation from God to man. Truth may come to us through the deep and clear intuitions of the mind itself, when its dominions are given to the inward sense, reposing in the sunlight of peace like a landscape beneath the eye. Then we know the truth or the falsehood of a proposition, not by reasoning out its results, but by the way it affects our higher sensibilities and by "intuitive beholding." A human nature entirely uncorrupt and unperverted would need no other revelation. Never darkened by sin, never overclouded with hereditary evil, it would receive the Divine light and reflect the Divine charms in childlike innocence, "lying in Abraham's bosom all the year." Nature would always be an open page, and matter always the true and living symbol of spirit;

for the "vis fervida mentis," the God glowing within, would be an ever-present interpreter to show a divine meaning in the humblest things. We infer from the earliest records, that such were the revelations made to primitive man. He had none other, and he needed none. His was the innocence which had no knowledge of good and evil by sorrowful experience, his the peace that had never been ruffled by sin. Consequently there was that constant revelation of God to man that comes through the inmost mind, and keeps it replenished with that mild wisdom which is better than sagacity, and those intuitions which are a surer guide than philosophy. No theologians were needed for creed-making, no logicians to prove a future life, since the voice of the Lord God was always audible, and the soul itself was full of immortality. The imagination, unpolluted by the imagery of sinful passion, unoccupied by the phantasma of error, might furnish a white ground on which heavenly things would copy themselves, and might become the picture-gallery of the glories of a higher world.

But when this state of innocence and purity is lost, the Divinity shines through our corruption with refracted and broken rays. Other instincts stir within us, and other voices speak than those which come from God. Yea, a long line of foul ancestry is speaking through us, and pouring the tides of its perverted life through our bosoms, tending thence to darken and to sensualize the reason. Instinct is no longer a safe guide, intuition no longer a revelation.

A man might take the combustion of his own passions for the glow of the God within him, and his own wildering fancies for the Divine Reason. Thus left to the downward impulsions that move him from within, he might reach that state of desolation which the prophet describes when darkness is put for light and evil for good. " He feedeth on ashes; a deceived heart hath turned him aside, that he cannot deliver his soul, nor say, Is there not a lie in my right hand?" Then it is that a Divine Rule of life, external to himself, becomes essential to his regeneration. He must have some sure standard out of himself by which all that is in him can be brought to the test. Hence another kind of revelation, one which comes from without, with those truths embodied and placed before us which had been darkened in the chaos within. The first revelation comes in the spontaneous workings of the faculties, and is the transfusion of heaven through the soul. The last comes through agencies external to ourselves, and lays a hand of authority upon us. It finds us in our defilement, in our gropings and wanderings; it hedges us round with restraints, it holds up before us the truth which we had lost and were toiling after in vain, and guides us through the rugged path of self-denial to its inward possession again. Let those make impulse their only law whose impulsions are the sure promptings of the Divinity. Let them make the inner light their only guide, whose reason has had no mildew from earth-born sentiments, that is, in whom human nature preserves all its purity and symmetry.

Those who know themselves know that their natures are no such media of Divine rays.

Hence the necessity of a revelation to the outward man also; and it must come down with its proofs as low as man has fallen. If he has fallen into sense, and become inlocked with sense, and shut in by his external perceptions, then the proofs of the revelation must come down into sense and find him there. Hence the Word made flesh attended with its signs in the natural world. Hence the Bible with its attestations of miracle, the embodiment of everlasting truth and of infallible rules for belief and practice. It comes at first, and commands us with the voice of God; it is our master, and not our servant; it may even be a hard master, and place us in a severe and painful school. But it has this peculiar proof both of its infolded Divinity and its renovating power, — that, received at first upon simple external evidence, the evidence grows more and more internal, till its pages become magically self-luminous. The path of self-denial into which it commands our roving feet, though at first steep and difficult, proves afterwards, like Milton's path of educational progress, " so smooth, so green, so full of goodly prospect, that the harp of Orpheus were not more charming."

In asserting this necessity of a revelation from without, we are saying nothing in derogation of the revelation from within. We are simply stating the facts of history and consciousness, when we say that the latter became insufficient, by reason of human degeneracy. Not that these inward revealings entirely cease, or can cease ; for in that case the outward revelation would be of no avail. It is to clarify this inner light, to restore it to its ancient effulgence, to afford an unerring standard by which to distinguish it from the flicker of strange fire within us, — it is for this that we have given us the Word written, and the Word made flesh. So, then, the unerring voice that speaks from the Bible interprets the voice that speaks in man, and distinguishes it from his own irregular frames and fancies, each harmonizing with the other, since each is a separate strain of the eternal melodies.

The instrumentality of the Scriptures in the work of human regeneration becomes manifest. It is this which gave to Protestantism all its power over other communions, as the front phalanx in the world's progress. And because Protestantism would not trust to its own first principle, but fell to Romanizing, it split into jarring and counteracting forces. To come in free contact with human souls, and act on them as the supreme energy, and lift them up into its broad and warm effulgence, the Bible must be the sole divine creed of the individual and the Church. Not until the inner revelation has been universally reproduced, must any body's interpretations of it come between the catechumen and his infallible guide. Not until truth is seen once more by intuitive beholding, and the outward revelation is superseded by the inward, can any communion of believers accept an inferior rule. For then they fall back into the same deadly peril that beset man before the revelation was received, that, namely, of mistaking human conceptions for the Divine reason, and human feelings and passions for the glow of God within. Because he was fallen, he needed a divine creed. Only because he is fallen, will he accept or impose any other. When intuition shall be unerring will human creeds become safe, and when they become safe they are useless.

Disregarding these obvious principles, Protestantism let go the Bible as the sole standard by which we are to gauge our intuitive sentiments and elevated private interpretations of the Bible in its place; and straightway it fell asunder into a thousand little popedoms, and hence the janglings of our Christian Babel. If its sects have attained to entire regeneration, (God help us if this chaos is such a state!) then, like man in Eden, they may dispense with creeds and Bibles together, since divine truth rewrites itself every day upon the heart. If they have not so attained, then their confessions are tinctured with the falsities of the natural man, and woe is to him who binds them about his neck, or writes them on the frontlets between his eyes.

In using the Sacred Scriptures, therefore, as a means of self-knowledge and regeneration, two essential conditions will become obvious. One has reference to the authority with which they should be received, and the other to the order in which they should be studied.

Their authority must be supreme and undivided.

We come away from the popedoms with which Christendom is distracted, whether the greater or the less ones, lest we be left on the low level where they are. We rise out of hearing of these earthly noises. We enter that still region that "lies away from broils." We ascend the sacred mount and talk with God alone. We leave the formulas which have no warmth in their blood and no speculation in their eyes, and come before the majestic form and the bright countenance of Truth itself. We escape the temptations of those who bring down the text and make it tally with church creeds in order to escape church censure and excision. We avoid the guilt of the sects who break up the awful form of truth into fragments and divide it among themselves, parting its garments among them, and casting lots for its vesture. Two alternatives are presented to us in the present state of the Christian world, — either to bring down the Divine Word into our own service and that of our denomination, and so turn it to private or partial ends, or let that Word bring us up into its own region of light and peace, and transfigure us amid its splendors. We must choose the latter.

Coming thus to the Divine Word, how or in what order shall we study it?

The Bible is a revelation *from* God, but it is not solely or even principally a revelation *of* God. It is also a revelation of man. Every possible condition of human nature is here painted in colors that live. All things pertaining to human experience, from the grossest naturalism to the highest spiritualism, are here quarried and brought out to view. Experience what you will, you shall find your experience here. Let your deepest want become known to you, and when you open these pages you shall find that want sending up its prevailing cry. In the Psalms alone humanity articulates its whole range of sentiments through all their compass of tones. The life of the Saviour, from his lowest humiliation to his final glorification, is the history of every possible conflict between the good and the evil, with the ensuing victory and glory. It is the majestic epic of humanity, where every stage of its progress is divinely pictured forth. Even the mystical books are full of human nature. As the spirit-world is the scene where man's imprisoned powers are unlocked and set free, so a description of that world is simply man opened. In the progress of our self-revealings we shall get a key to the sense of the Apocalypse itself. It is (we suggest) the inmost mind led forth on a theatre where there is no stint to its ongoings. Its gorgeous cloudland is none other than man uncovered. The judgment day which the Scriptures describe does not reveal the wrath of God superimposed upon the creature, but a development out of human nature, the unrolling of all its secrets into day. The Paradise of God, adorned with the tree of life, and threaded with streams of water, is not the sensual heaven of Orientalism, but rather the state where purified souls are surrounded with their own lovely creations. So we say, first, Divine revelation is a revelation of man, and according to his upward or downward tendencies it is an apocalypse of glory, or an apocalypse of woe.

Then, again, it is a revelation of God. It is the Divine mind and will unveiled toward man. It is the Eternal Wisdom brought out to view in an all-harmonizing system of doctrines, calculated to touch man's palsied powers, and make them live again. It is infinite truth unrolled in its order to the eye and the intellect, which else had been apprehended by an inward sense, and been perceived by intuitive beholding. So that the life of God and the life of man are both revealed here, — the former acting upon the latter, seeking to purify it and bring it into harmony with itself. The Bible, therefore, is an exhibition of the things hidden within us, — hidden often far beneath the reach of our consciousness. Deep in our souls there are the same twofold forces, — the Divine life and the human, with their strivings and interactions; only, as we become degenerate and live chiefly in externals, these things within us are seen dimly or not at all; but the Bible holds them up before us again on a page that is open and illumined.

All this suggests to us the way and the order in which the Scriptures should be used and studied, as aids in our regeneration. We may read them only in the order of chapter and verse, with a whole lumber-house of commentaries to help us, and yet know little or nothing of what is in them. We should read them in the order of our own experiences and needs. These are developed in succession as we advance in the life of regeneration. Divine Providence, whenever we give ourselves into his hands like little children, leads us along through the circuit of our self-revealings, so as to make us feel each in its time our inmost needs, and that drawing of the Holy Spirit towards those truths by which these needs shall be satisfied. For this reason the word of God is called bread, water, implying that it is to be sought for when we hunger and when we thirst. It has doctrines adapted to every possible change of our life, and themes which at special times are urged upon us with special power, and hold our attention awake. If we seek it for the sole end of self-purification, searching for the truth which our present condition requires and our nature craves, we shall be drawn to the pages where that truth waits for us, and it shall rise on our vision with clearer and clearer blaze, as the astronomer sought the new planet, and wept for joy when it crossed over the glass. For the Bible being a revelation of humanity, every aspect of it, as it changes from shade into light, is painted with the Divine pencil upon its leaves. Every needful doctrine will meet us at every new stage, and when we have turned it into conduct, another will rise on our sight. And so star after star will come down into our sky, and Christianity be given to us as an ever-unfolding system, its doctrines pouring on our path their blending and beautiful rays.

We will now illustrate by three specifications the value of this mode of using the Divine oracles.

Perhaps the first question which an earnest mind is called to grapple with, is the question of innate depravity. As a question of speculative theology, presented to us from without, it may be settled any way by reading works on original sin or the dignity of man, according as one's fancies or ecclesiastical relations may happen to be. But let the question come up from within, and press for an answer till it hinders us from sleep. It comes sooner or later to almost every one not utterly lost in worldliness; sometimes in vague dissatisfactions with present attainment; sometimes in longings after peace; sometimes in the unrealized anticipations of our dreaming childhood, when the dews that sparkled on the foliage in the first golden light have all disappeared, and naught remains but the sweat and heat and burden of the day; sometimes in the avenging consciousness of God's inly pervading and broken laws. Now if the inquirer settles this question by the "standard works" or the popular preachers of his church, he will most assuredly fall into the ruts of some provincial theology, and follow the unceasing round of its creaking wains. But if he comes freely and freshly to the Divine Word, with an earnest beseeching that his own heart may be unveiled, he will find that word quick and powerful, shooting darts of light through the deepest places of his soul. There are two classes of passages where the whole matter of human nature and human wants is treated at large. There is the narrative portion and the ethical. In the former, man is revealed historically and experimentally; in the latter, by that divine logic which pierces the heart and rends its gauzy sophistries away. There is everywhere a basis of fact, and on this basis rests the work of divine argumentation. Large portions of the Old Testament are human nature exposed. The Psalms are its deep, spontaneous utterances. In the New we see it wrestling with its foes in the desert of temptation, or bending low under its sorrowful burden in the shades of the garden. As specimens of the ethical portion, take the Sermon on the Mount, the discourse with Nicodemus, or Paul's delineation of the higher and lower nature. And everywhere, out of heaven and out of Christ, are revealings of the Divine nature, giving us gleams of an untold and unimagined purity that pierce the darkness of our hearts and make the darkness visible.

Another question is sure to arise, and another want is sure to be felt, — that of atonement for sin. When this question comes up from without, men invent theories of the Divine government and go off into endless logomachies. When it comes up from within, and urges us to the Divine record, we find our deepest experience arrayed before us, and the truth that speaks to our condition. There is the narrative of the coming, life, death, resurrection, ascension, and glorification of the Son of Man, and his second coming as the Comforter, to suffuse the penitent heart with the sweet elixir of peace, — a constellation of truths under whose guidance we cannot miss our way. Then the ethics of the subject of atonement are set forth in the parable of the prodigal, — itself a comprehensive and lovely theology. The facts of our consciousness are here drawn out in the clearest array. Every step of our progress from the city of Destruction to the city of God is here mapped out before us. Here is our fall and desolation. Here is repentance, conversion, and reconciliation, when we come home again, and the father embraces and kisses his child, and puts the best robe upon him, — even as the great Father gives to his renewed and reconciled children the clothing of new and heavenly moralities.

There are seasons when the themes of immortality come home to our bosoms in such shapes that they will not away at our bidding. When the chair is vacant, and the chamber is still, and affection is weeping at the bier, we dread the mockery of delusions. We want realities.

It will be obvious, on a moment's thought, how closely this subject connects itself with human nature and human redemption, and that to reveal man here is to reveal his state hereafter. When we form to ourselves artificial theories spun from the metaphysics of the Church, we do not lay hold of the life to come, nor see the sublime pneumatology which the Bible unfolds. To open man's book of life, is to break the seals from the word. If heaven and hell are not arbitrary appointments, but man uncovered, and his powers led out and dramatized on an ampler field, then our souls are openings into another world, and from this outlook we see adown the long avenues, and their solemn forms come before us as in a mystic glass. Let this subject come up in its order, after human nature with its deep-working laws has been revealed to us, and a "theory of the future life" based on indubitable fact would be developed; the letter of Scripture would shine white as the light, bursting with the revealing mysteries of an hereafter. False and artificial theories of man connect themselves indissolubly with false and artificial theories of a future life, for the future life is in fact our present life concealed and folded up. The land of immortality becomes baseless and spectral. The beings with which the technical theologies have peopled it, are any thing but men and women. No wonder the question is anxiously raised, "Shall we know our friends hereafter?" Who could recognize among those winged and shadowy beings "the old, familiar faces"?

We are burdened with a sense of the importance of the theme we are handling, so deep, that we fail to transfer it to our pages. We believe that all our costly apparatus of interpretation does little more as yet than touch the letter of the Divine volume, but that its spirit is yet to break upon us as never before, and that the day which Robinson foresaw is yet to dawn. For thickly as the theologians have woven their web around this book, like the silkworm spinning her threads, "till she clouds herself all o'er," yet even now, when touched with reverent hand, there come sparkles from its muffled truths, as from jars surcharged with electric fire. The wants of these times urge us to seek with fresh diligence, and with new preparation of heart, the responses of the sacred oracles. Let us leave the sects in the oblivious past. At least let us get out of these prisons, into which light comes in scant allowance, and only through stained glass. With all our varied culture, our systems of education and our popular literature, still comes the question from earnest and famished natures, Who will show us any good? They go to this and that gathering for social stimulus; to "popular preachers," who out of their own eloquence and ingenuity attempt to supply food for the soul, and still the soul hungers and thirsts. Commentators attempt to open the Divine Word, but it will not open at their bidding. They smite the rock, but still the soul hungers and thirsts. Each sect sets forth its manuals of doctrine, and makes out its case, but still there is a waiting and a pause. We have religious excitements, and machinery to keep them up. Those that work the machinery get out of breath, and then it stops, and there is a waiting and a pause. Some go back to Rome for rest and shelter, "like a child seeking nourishment and repose on the cold bosom of its dead mother." All the while, the book out of which light is to come lies upon our shelves, — ready to yield its revelations, not to some costly apparatus of interpreters, but to the humble and seeking mind; ready to give light when restored to its ancient authority in the Church, and the usurping creeds of the logomachists are taken away. Let the inquirer forsake these, and steal an hour every day from the literature that surfeits, but does not satisfy and save. And when the great problems of life and destiny come up each in its turn, and press painfully upon him, let him not give over till the truth stands clear to the intellect, and through that pours a mellow sunshine into his soul. Then the truth lost shall emerge anew and become intuition again. Then the inner folds of the heart shall be laid open, ere come the solemn disclosures of the judgment time.

CHAPTER VII.

CONFLICT AND VICTORY.

"The language of the Bible harmonizes with all human experience, in declaring that all progress implies effort, resistance, combat; — but there are intervals of peace, — intervals when the battle of that day is won and the wearied soldier rests and rejoices; intervals when the climbing pilgrim has reached a mountain-top, and while he breathes the sweet freshness of the air, he looks back upon his nights of darkness and his days of toil, and around upon a world now glowing with beauty because the love that fills it is for that hour unveiled, and upward to a sky from which the clouds have melted or else give back the sunshine in golden light, and forward to the distant and loftier summits where peace has a more abiding home." — PARSONS'S ESSAYS.

WE have described the antagonistic forces which struggle for the possession of human nature. There is hereditary evil, with its passions and its brood of lies. There is the effluent Spirit of God always immanent in human nature, always claiming it as his own province of light and love. There is the uprising world of darkness, with all its tempting fiends; there are the bending heavens, with their guardian angels; and the field of conflict is the soul of man. The alternations of defeat and victory, until the final catastrophe takes place, constitute the solemn drama of humanity. Mankind in all ages have been conscious of this conflict, and the highest achievement which any nation's literature hath ever made, has been worthily to conceive and picture it forth. One of the oldest poems in Hindoo literature is a noble epic which sets forth in mythical form this sacred war. God becomes incarnate in order to combat the kingdom of evil, whose genii were overrunning the kingdom of light, and the Christian reader is startled as he goes along, to find Christian ideas antedating the greater portion of his own Bible, and warming and inspiring the oldest profane literature in the world.* With this conflict Divine revelation opens, and with this it closes. The conflict begins amid the blooming scenery of Eden, and it winds up in the gorgeous visions of St. John. Almost every book describes an act in this fearful drama. In man's deepest consciousness, read sometimes clearly and sometimes dimly, is the subject-matter of a Paradise Lost and a Paradise Regained, which the seers and bards of humanity have struggled to articulate distinctly in prophecy and song. Only when the things of immortality become mere matters of tradition, and not subjective realities, man conceives this drama as enacted in some far off and imaginary heavens, and not where alone it can be found, — in himself.

This drama has a twofold catastrophe, for either of these powers may be victorious. If we welcome the powers of light and coöperate with them, their dominion enlarges till it comprehends our entire nature. All evil powers are driven out, all corrupt

* Heeren's Asia. See his critique upon the Ramayana.

proclivities cease. The conflict is over and the issue is peace. Or we may side with the evil forces, and then their victory will be sure. Not all at once, for the mind still opens inward towards a brighter sphere, and receding voices for a long time will talk along the avenues. But a necessity lies upon every man either to obey the truth or else reject it; for if not obeyed, it fills the soul with torturing memories, and gives a foresight of retribution until its light is is excluded. The spirit that speaks within must either be obeyed or "grieved" away. Therefore all selfish and sinful indulgence, all worldly living, is the coming on of the shadows of night. God and immortality become the traditions, if not the fables, of olden time. The world of spirit is shadowy and phantasmic, while the world of sense is solid and real. Towards God and the things that are above, the mind is darkened and closed. Towards sense and things below, with all their sorceries and seductions, the mind is alive and open wide. The evil powers are victorious, and the issue is religious insensibility and spiritual death. "They make a solitude and they call it peace."

The path of our regenerate life, therefore, is the strait and climbing and rugged pathway of Christian obedience. When once our book of life has been opened to us, every evil disposition that stirs within us is to be resisted, mortified, and slain. As fast as the old man is crucified, the new man is put on. Every lust that is denied, is driven out by "the expulsive power of a new affection." As fast as the kingdom of darkness recedes, the kingdom of light comes on. This is not the sole work of the closet or the Sabbath day. In our daily walk, in our minutest affairs, are the occasions found when the temptation without brings to light the evil within, and they call and answer to each other. Then the evil stands out naked and undisguised, and we grapple with it on a fair and open field. Thus all the desires of the natural man "come full circle," are successively denied and repressed, and the corresponding dispositions of the spiritual man beam forth in the most external life, and clothe themselves in new and heavenly moralities. Every temptation resisted is a defeat of the powers of evil, and every such defeat makes our next victory more certain and easy. And when our most unremembered deeds are redolent of spontaneous and angel sympathies, God reigns in our most external as well as our most internal man. He is first, and he is last. He reigns in our central being, and in its remotest circuit, and therefore in all that interspaces these two. But the work is not complete so long as any combination of circumstances can stir a passion within us which is to be denied and crucified.

This conflict between the passions of the natural man and the angel band of pure affections, between self and God struggling for supremacy in the soul, is such, that the perturbations are sometimes long and fearful, and the soul seems to itself to be driven to and fro on the billows of an angry sea. It may even be such, that this subjective world of contending forces may fling the shadows of its own shapes upon outward things, and the individual shall see out of him an image of the warfare that rages within. Luther's temptations were of this kind, when the fiend that first took shape and consistence in his own passions seemed to pass into objectivity, and fling his grim shadows upon the wall. Bunyan's temptations passed into this stage, when the calls and responses between the tempter without and the evil within were so loud and strong, that some one seemed to be sending his voice after him, and he would look round and say, Who calls? And again the deep waking voices of God's spirit were so distinct and clear, that they seemed as articulate and audible as if they fell on the outward ear.* So the strength that comes to us during the struggle may be such, and the peace of victory won may be so clear-shining and heavenly, that they shall seem to fling their splendors into the external world, and overlay the appearances of the senses. Thus in the darkest Gethsemanes of life the angel may appear from heaven to strengthen the sufferer, and when the tempter is driven away and the struggle is over, the sunshine that follows may be the brightness flung from the wings of seraphim. That is a shallow philosophy, and one whose plummet never sounded the deeps of humanity, which ascribes all this to fantasy, and then thinks the mystery explained. For such are the openings of the internal mind towards a spirit-realm,

* See Bunyan's Life, prefixed to Pilgrim's Progress.

that natures extremely susceptible shall not only receive its influences, but, in moments of intense mental action, have its images formed in their perceptions; and then the great conflict on which hang such momentous issues, the conflict of the good with the evil, the true with the false, is shadowed forth externally, and the moral battle paints itself upon the canvas of the senses.

Fortunately, however, most men have not these extremely, susceptible natures, and corrupt inclinations may be denied, as they come successively into the consciousness, without these violent perturbations. The path of our regeneration is open and plain. It is simple self-denial, until there is no self to be denied. This is never accomplished without painful vigils and struggles, and persevering toil, however smoothly our external affairs may flow on. There are those of ripe experience, of high Christian attainment, of that heavenly-mindedness which is always serene and unclouded as the upper sky. But all this did not come of itself. Always when the internal experience of such persons is disclosed to us, we find that they reached those summits of peace through conflicts and watchings, that sometimes chased repose from their pillows. There are those with whom this work begins with the first dawnings of reason, — who, like Samuel, hear the voice of the Lord in childhood, and follow it devoutly, — who never suffer inborn corruption to come forth into voluntary life, — who therefore need not be converted in order to be regenerated and saved; but whose characters grow into forms of Christian piety and grace, as the palm-tree rises graceful and majestic amid the stillness of the forest. With them the struggle is less severe; every victory is easy, and their Christian course is a continuous ovation. Conscience always obeyed becomes unerring and clear, sweeter to hear than a song at evening, its voice a constant "Well done!" from the indwelling Spirit of God. If there is any thing in the universe fitted to awaken emotions of the morally sublime and beautiful, like this unfolding of childhood into the conscientious young man or woman, we do not know what it is, — childhood leading a charmed life, walking through the furnace while the flames play innocuous around. We may find its image and representation in nature, but we can find nothing half so lovely. I have seen the planet of evening, when her disc was nearly obscure, — "the new moon with the old moon in her arm," — and she seemed little else than a dark mass hanging in the sky. But she turns towards the sun, and a brighter crescent appears; it grows larger and encroaches upon the line of darkness, till she emerges complete in light, and rides in full beauty along the plains of heaven. Such is childhood emerging out of hereditary corruption, not through the spasms and agonies of repentance and conversion, but through growth in that grace that never fails, but always enlarges till it comprehends the whole man, and he reflects the Divine light and the Divine charms in complete beauty and glory.

But it is the shame of our Christian education and

Christian example, that there are few such cases as these. The way of our regeneration lies through bitter repentances and death-struggles for victory, and perhaps at the end of our mortal course we find the victory but half gained. And yet we would not represent that the Christian life is only a life of struggle. There are intervals of sunshine and peace, when we rest upon our arms and contemplate the fields we have won, and the affluent dominions we are yet to gain. The region of eternal rest is not reached through a path of incessant upward toil. We go from one height to another, as hills rise above hills, and on every height gained we enjoy its partial peace, and in our breathing-time we sing victorious songs. There are seasons when our wrong propensities are quiescent, and we rest from our labor until temptation wakes them up and the conflict begins anew. And when one of these enemies is destroyed, we have the peace of victory till another comes in sight, all the while rejoicing in our faith in Him who is our shield and buckler, and who gives us at these intervals the earnest of everlasting rest.

CHAPTER VIII.

THE MEDIATOR.

> "The few pale stars had vanished from the sky;
> There was no moon, but blackness over all
> Dense as the cloak of death, without relief,
> Or hope of change, — a visible despair:
> Then the retiring darkness gave to view
> A lucid sphere enveloped in the gloom;
> Sudden, effulgent, glorious, it burst,
> As if a sun were born at midnight deep.
> Radius-like bent round the brow of Christ
> It shone, the promised DAY-SPRING FROM ON HIGH."

THE theology of the New Testament involves three leading ideas, all of which centre in the person of Jesus Christ.

First, there is a perfect and glorified HUMAN NATURE, exhibiting in its changes from its humiliation to its exaltation all the possible virtues, graces, and excellences that belong to our human condition.

Secondly, there is the DIVINE NATURE in its paternal benignity, infinite wisdom, and universal and unchanging love, contrasting with the dark and partial conceptions of God which prevailed among Jews and Gentiles.

Thirdly, there is the UNION of these two in Jesus Christ, so that in him are revealed at the same time a perfect humanity and the all-perfect Divinity.

All classes of Christians receive these three ideas, though not in the same combinations. All believe that the New Testament reveals the perfect man. All believe that it reveals the perfect God, the Universal Father. All believe that in Jesus Christ God and humanity were united. It is when they come to discuss the *mode* of this connection, whether by inspiration, by indwelling, or by hypostatic union, that differences begin to appear. We are not going to follow out these subtilties. "That way madness lies."

Keeping close to our main purpose, however, and hoping to draw the reader along with us, we premise that it is no example of mere human nature, however sublimated and exalted, that satisfies our wants as sinful men. No finite power and influence can create us anew. No models of human virtue, however pure and perfect, are to regenerate and save us. Rather do they dazzle and mock us with ideals which we can never realize ourselves. I may fix on them my earnest and despairing gaze; but there aloft they shine and shine in vain, giving me gleams of a region of purity and peace which I cannot climb to, and which fall upon my unsunned and frozen nature like the shimmer of moonbeams upon a mass of snow. Christ has placed before me an example of human perfection, and told me to follow in his steps. And is that all? If that *be* all, it were like standing on the shore and helping a drowning man by merely shouting to him to rise and walk the waves. In our fallen, sinful state, it is not first and chiefly an example that we want. We want God. We want Divine succor and influence, coming within us with creative power, not primarily to bring us into conformity with some model that is placed before us, but to revive the Divine image within us, so that by its own radiation it shall produce around us the halo of all Christian virtues and graces.

Whatever, then, may be the mode of union between the human and the Divine in the person and history of Jesus Christ, — and we shrink from applying the scalpel of our metaphysics to the Divine nature, — this one truth stands bold and prominent in the entire history of the incarnation, that the human was so overlaid, controlled, and possessed by the Divine, that the Saviour is without reserve "God with us." The Divine inlays all his words and actions, so that they are the undoubted expositions of the Eternal Wisdom and Love. The New Testament writers are careful to inform us that the man Christ Jesus had no human father, but that the Holy Spirit itself descended into this world and took its normal clothing of flesh and blood and its expression in the human form. They put this fact in the foreground of the Christian theology, for by this fact they make the Author of Christianity not an inspired prophet, but a Divine Man. The prophet is inspired to utter his message, and that done he is like other men. Christ was not inspired after birth, but the effluence of the Divine nature formed the inmost principle of his natural being, so that his most common words and works had their ground in the ingenerating Divinity. The natural life of Christ became hence the *expression of God*, and the influence proceeding from him the effusion of the Holy Spirit.

St. John asserts the same truth in describing the Divine Word made flesh, that is, brought down into the conditions of mortal existence and clothed in human form. He is asserting the ground of Christ's plenary authority and wisdom, and this he does by describing these fleshly surroundings as enfolding the Divine wisdom, life within life, — the infinite become visible in the finite, not by being superinduced upon Christ by special gift, but by forming the inmost principle of his natural being. Nothing less than this satisfies the record of the supernatural conception by Matthew, or of the Divine incarnation by John. Indeed, these two chapters aside, nothing short of the fact which they describe explains that phenomenal Divine life which the whole history of Jesus brings to view. Both his words and his works are quite inexplicable without it. " He that hath seen me hath seen the Father, and how sayest thou then, Show us the Father ? " " The words which I speak unto you I speak not of myself, but the Father that dwelleth in me, he doeth the works." The finite human nature received from Mary was obsequious to the inmost Divinity, was its living transparency which served to symbolize and copy it out.

Without attempting, therefore, any rigid or exact analysis, in which we might perhaps lose the company of the reader, we trust that he will approach with us in reverent mood the sublime and central truth to which we are coming. We lay off all the theories of the schoolmen pertaining to the mode of union between God and Christ. We forget all the disputes of the sects upon this question. We recognize the fact that such a union, though it may involve mysteries, involves no contradictions. We do not stop at what is mortal and finite in the fact of the Divine incarnation; we do not even see the finite, but look through it as we look through glass to see the sun; and then the Divine nature unveils itself to our longing vision, and out of Jesus Christ comes the unclouded blaze of the Godhead! *

The practical bearing of this truth on the state of the world and the regeneration of man soon becomes obvious. It is obvious in many respects, but principally from the fact of A NEW DISPENSATION OF THE SPIRIT THROUGH THE MEDIATOR. Taking the fact

---

* We are confident that we have here stated substantially the doctrine, not only of the New Testament writers, but of the ante-Nicene fathers and the Nicene Council itself, concerning the nature of Christ. The modern doctrine of a distinction of *persons* in the Godhead did not enter at all into the Arian controversy. That was the invention of a later age. The question between Arius and his opposers was, whether Christ is begotten out of God, and therefore ὁμοούσιος, consubstantial with the Father, or whether he was formed out of nothing by the creative power of God. Arius affirmed the latter doctrine. His opposers the former. The Nicene Council decided against Arius, and (as we think) in accordance with the New Testament writers, especially Matthew, Luke, and John, in their introductory chapters. See Murdock's Mosheim, Vol. I. pp. 287 – 290. Also Stuart's article on Sabellianism in the Biblical Repository.

which three of the Evangelists have placed so conspicuously in the foreground of their history, that Jesus Christ was begotten of the Holy Spirit, which thus became the inmost principle of his natural being, it would hence result that the influence emanating from him is the Holy Spirit itself. And this truth shines with great fulness through all the narrative that follows. It was conspicuous at his baptism. The Evangelist evidently does not mean to say that the natural heavens were opened, and that the symbolic dove descended out of *them*. Rather does he mean that the heavens opened from within; their light streaming outward and investing the person of the Son of God with their encircling glory, in which glory were seen to play the wings of the holy dove, emblem of that Holy Spirit which, from being the inmost principle of his nature, was becoming also its outermost manifestation, its Last as well as First.

In that memorable discourse of Jesus with his disciples at the table of the last supper, he promises to send them the Comforter, "whom," he adds, "the world cannot receive, because it seeth him not, neither knoweth him. But ye know him; for HE DWELLETH WITH YOU, and shall be *in* you." The Comforter is synonymous with the Holy Spirit. It dwelt *with* the disciples in the person of the Son of God, but not yet had it penetrated the darkness of their minds. Not yet had the world recognized its presence, immersed in its superstitions and idolatries. But this Holy Spirit was to come to them with other demonstrations than those made through its fleshly coverings. One of the grand results which the death of Christ was to accomplish, was to bring the Holy Ghost by taking away the hiding of its power. The interposition of a mortal body between the spiritual Christ and his followers, was as a cloud that concealed the sun and intercepted its rays. The Comforter was *with* them, but not *in* them. He had unfolded to them an infinite system of truth, but its doctrines lay cold and dead in their memories. The seed had been deposited in the soil, but not yet had come the warm sunshine and the spring gales.

The import of our Saviour's language afterwards to his disciples hence becomes apparent. "It is expedient for you that I go away; for *if I go not away, the Comforter will not come unto you;* but if I depart, I will send him unto you." * As if he had said, "Though I am with you in this mortal body, yet I am separated from you. I withdraw from your sight, that I may get nearer to your spirit. I can come to you out of the immortal state, and out of my glorified body, as I cannot come to you out of these environments of mortality." This is the reason why the Holy Ghost was not given *before* Jesus *was glorified.*† Out of the material body and through the clogs of the senses, the influences that came from Jesus did not reach the inmost hearts of his followers; but these clogs being removed, and coming to his disciples from the spiritual side, those in-

* John xvi. 7

† John vii. 39.

fluences might be felt with new demonstrations of power. Such was the promise made by Christ to his disciples, — the promise of a new gift of the Holy Spirit: — "I go away that I may come again."

How wonderful was the fulfilment! At the first meeting of the Saviour with his disciples, *after his death and resurrection*, the Evangelist says, "he breathed on them, and saith unto them, Receive ye the Holy Ghost." But the fulfilment is witnessed in its most memorable results about forty days after his crucifixion, namely, at the Feast of Pentecost. The disciples had assembled with vague anticipations of the promised gift. At length the influence came. Their souls are suddenly swept by the breezes of God's spirit, which elevated all their powers of conception, emotion, and utterance. The truths that lay cold in their memories now glow like living coals, reminding them of the promise that the Comforter should "bring all things to their remembrance." Those timid men, who forsook their Master at the cross, now confront danger and death with loosened tongues, and with tidings of a world's salvation. But the gift is not to the disciples alone; it is the inheritance of the rising Church, and its first day's evidence is the conversion of three thousand souls. "This Jesus," exclaims Peter in the midst of this triumphal scene, "hath God raised up, whereof we are all witnesses; and having received of the Father the promise of the Holy Ghost, *he hath shed forth this, which ye now see and hear.*"

May we not pause here a moment, and contemplate

the summit of Calvary as a scene of triumph! The enemies of the Saviour thought they were taking the most potent means to cover him with defeat and ruin. They were the very means he had taken into his plan of success and victory. They thought that, by killing the body and putting it out of sight, this new religion would be swept from the earth. He knew that, when free of the body, he should have access to the minds of his followers by means more efficacious than those of language. They thought that, when the body was bruised in pieces, all was at an end. He knew that this was tearing away the chief hindrance of his power. They thought that, by killing the body, they put Christ out of the way. He knew that this would bring him more completely into the midst of his disciples, yea, into the heart of humanity, as that power which should shake down old dynasties and change the face of the world.

We come now to a clear apprehension of the meaning of Paul, in that large class of passages in which he ascribes so much efficacy to the influence of the living Christ. It is a most remarkable fact, that, while the modern Church ascribes the chief efficacy in man's redemption to the death of Christ, Paul ascribes it to his LIFE AND RESURRECTION. "If Christ be not *raised*, your faith is vain; *ye are yet in your sins*." His sufferings and death are of no avail to cancel your sins, except as a means of exaltation to that sphere, whence his spirit operates with new power in cleansing your sins away. Again:

"If, while we were yet sinners, we were reconciled to God by the death of his Son, *much more*, being reconciled, WE SHALL BE SAVED BY HIS LIFE."* And yet again he speaks of "Christ that died"; but checking himself, "yea, *rather*, that is RISEN AGAIN, and who maketh intercession for us."† We may well stand with dissolving hearts in view of the spectacle on Calvary. But our repentance were "a most unprevailing woe," were it not that, from the heavens to which Christ is exalted, the life of God out of his glorified humanity passes daily into our hearts to create them anew. The Apostle thus makes the resurrection of Christ the fundamental doctrine of the gospel system: "If thou shalt confess with thy mouth the Lord Jesus, and believe in thy heart that God *raised him from the dead*, thou shalt be saved."‡ The Apostle most clearly does not mean, by the resurrection of Christ, the reanimation of the natural body. He means that whole process through which he ascended out of mortality into the glorified state. He means by it the putting off of these limitations of flesh and sense, and the putting on of that spiritual form in which he came anew to his disciples, and "shed forth" the Holy Ghost into his rising Church and into the hearts of all his followers. And when he describes the Christ of consciousness, the Christ that is "formed within us," we do not understand him to be using language idly and vaguely. Rather does he describe that im-

---

* Rom. v. 10. † Ibid. viii 34. ‡ Ibid. x. 9.

age of Christ formed in the Christian heart by those rays of Divine light that fall into it out of the glorified nature of the great Redeemer.

We would not by any means deny the influences that come to us from the life of Christ in the flesh, or his death on Calvary, considered as an example of sublime virtue and majestic patience. Doubtless we are guided by looking at that example. Doubtless, by a contemplation of that great sacrifice, that all-consecrating devotion of the outward and the finite to the God within, we get the lesson of self-consecration, and learn how we ought to live. Doubtless, the sweet, forgiving spirit, which at the crucifixion beamed out through the convulsions of nature, like sunbeams struggling through the cloud and fringing the wings of the storm, has found its way into many hearts in hours of tender communion. But if Christ had not been *raised*, we had been "yet in our sins." His death is efficacious as the rending away of that veil which hung between him and the hearts of men, as breaking down the chief obstacle in the way of pouring his life in warm, full tides into the bosom of humanity. Paul, had he seen Christ in the flesh only, would perhaps have joined hands with his murderers. But when he saw him amid the revealing glories of another sphere, he was smitten to the earth, and cried, "Lord, what wilt thou have me to do?" And though no such vision was given to all the disciples, yet not less was his Divine Person close to them, insphering them in its own life and light, whose influence, breathing through the soul, was everywhere felt as the gales of this spring-time of Christianity.

The history of the first triumphs of the gospel is entirely inexplicable on any ordinary principles, and might well baffle a profounder man than Mr. Gibbon. Put yourself in the presence of these early preachers, and witness the results! Some reasoners have attempted to account for the rapid spread of Christianity in those times, by the power which the first disciples had of working miracles, — such as healing the sick, raising the dead, and the like. Let any such reasoner read the Acts of the Apostles in reference to this matter, and he will find the facts against him. A few plain men, with their simple message, begin to speak to men more rude than themselves, immersed in the night of paganism. Almost at the name of Jesus of Nazareth, new emotions rush through their hearts, and new conceptions rise in their minds, and go forth into spontaneous utterance, as from tongues that are tipped with fire.* The Holy Ghost "fell on them that heard the word," so that these preachers were themselves "astonished" at that hidden power in whose motions, the wills of men were swayed like reeds that bend before the wind. It was obvious throughout, that a sphere of Divine Life had come nearer to the earth, and through Christianity was touching the human will; and when the veil of sense was rolled away, as it sometimes was, and these men were permitted to have gleams

* See Acts x. 44 – 47.

of the new agencies that were moving upon human nature, they saw the glorified form of the risen Christ, out of which came shafts of Divine fire. Such was the introversion of the dying Stephen, of the persecuting Saul, and of the prophet of Patmos, into that sphere whose radiances were piercing the consciousness of men and infusing unwonted energies. The miraculous works which attended the first spread of Christianity were not so much causes as effects, being demonstrations into the sphere of sense and matter of a power that was shaking the inner sphere of thought and will, and turning its ancient foundations out of course.

We regard this new spiritual influence as the peculiar inheritance of the Christian Church. It was not the first disciples alone who were brought into this peculiar relation to the risen Lord. "The promise is unto you and your children, and to all that are afar off, even as many as the Lord our God shall call."* That the promise made by Jesus to be with his people "*always*, even to the end of the world," is of the same import as the promise made to the twelve to come to them again as the Comforter, is, we think, quite evident, both from the terms of the promise, and from its fulfilment in the course of Christian history. It is this new dispensation of the Holy Spirit, which makes Christianity the sovereign energy in renovating society, and changing the condition of mankind. Other forms of faith

* Acts ii. 39.

have embodied important moral truths, but for want of this vitalizing influence they all wane to their extinction. Jesus Christ was announced as that being who should not baptize with water, — a cleansing merely of the outward life, — but who should "BAPTIZE WITH THE HOLY GHOST AND WITH FIRE." Within the circle of Christendom, as in a luminous centre, is the risen and personal Christ, out of whose exalted nature comes, as out of the fulness of the Godhead, a life made diffusive through the hearts of men. This is the reason why within this circle come ever new undulations of energy, breaking into the belt of darkness that surrounds it. Hence every new season of refreshing has been a new coming of Christ, and every period of wide-spread renovation has been with a new consciousness of the personal presence of, and of personal relations to, the Divine Redeemer. The history of the Protestant Reformation, and more especially of the Methodist renovation of the last century, will verify our statement. And it is quite as remarkable, that no sect or body of men that has received Christianity only as an abstract system of faith and morals, and its Founder only as an historical person, leaving out the living Christ as the ever-present medium of the Divine energy, has ever won for itself a place in history, as one of the great motive forces of human progress. Such sects have only a feeble and transitory existence. They fall into dead works, collapse and die. They are the Ebionites of ecclesiastical annals.

The bearing of this theme on individual regeneration and progress is of transcendent importance. We make our appeal to the experience of the reader. When you have sought communion with God without a Mediator, have you not found your idea of God dissipated and fading off into Pantheism, till God becomes an evanescent spirit, that "rolls through all things," but from whose living Person comes no Divine energy that wakes up and concentrates all your faculties, and whose conscious presence is your comfort and joy? And has not the religious sentiment, from being the motive power to great sacrifices and achievements, sunk away towards an aimless and dreamy sentimentalism, or perhaps what is worse, a worldly insensibility and unbelief. Then Christ is an historical character, not the ever-present Mediator, in whom God is seen reconciling the world unto himself. Away back in the past he appears, as a beautiful pattern of excellence; you reach after it, but you never get nearer to it; and when you try to forsake your sins and escape from spiritual death, you seem to make no progress, like a man escaping from a monster in a dream. You find that the ordinances of religion are soon without spirit and meaning. Why join a Church which has no living head except in a figure of speech? Why keep celebrating the death of one who has been dead two thousand years? Restore the doctrine of the One Divine Mediator to the Church and to your own soul, and see the change! Not a Mediator who comes in between you and God to divert his punishments, but out of whom comes God's all-renewing spirit in unceasing waves of light and love, — the Mediator of the Church in the day of her bridal glories. Then you have the "Christ that died, — yea, *rather*, that is risen again," — the Saviour who appeared to St. John, and whose countenance is as the sun shining in his strength, who is present in his ordinances in a higher sense than the Papist dreams of, and who comes anew into your soul to make his truth alive and glowing.

There are, we think, pretty clear indications that the present is a period that lies on the eve of one of those great renewals of the Church and of society which are called eras. Two things there are which raise the expectation that another wave out of the eternal energy is circling towards us, and even breaking upon the shores of time.

First, there is the indisputable fact that the old forms of belief and modes of operation have done about all they can do in renewing society. Misery and sin lie around the Church in solid masses, yea, within its inclosures; and the conning of its litanies, and the recital of its creeds, have no more effect in penetrating these masses, than have moonbeams in melting the rock. What have the great world's affairs to do with the spells that are muttered in churches? And yet the great world's affairs are going wrong. Doctrines clung to with the most tenacity have no intelligible reference to practice, and the practice is much the same whether the doctrines are assented to or not. Reformers go forth in their own name, but their fierce maledictions return back upon them, verifying anew the principle, that he cannot cast out demons who is possessed of one himself. At the same time, — and this is a second and most auspicious sign, — there is among men of earnest and reverent moods a pause and an expectation, as if they heard a divine voice just becoming articulate and audible, — coming, not out of the old creeds, but out of the Divine Word and out of the most interior consciousness of men, and prophesying of the things that are yet to be. They would say, and they *do* say, that our traditionary and tangled theologies do not give to them the living Christ, — the Christ that came to John in Patmos, or that broke upon Paul and arrested him with overwhelming glories. Though his death is celebrated on sacrament days, they yet feel that Christ is not dead! On the other hand, a new Christology is being born out of the warm love of pious hearts, — as if the same Comforter were coming again and drawing all to himself. "What power divine diffuseth far this tenderness of mind?" Whence this growing consciousness of the Saviour's personal presence as the luminous centre of his Church, and the living power in the heart of the disciple, unless it be a new fulfilment of the promise, "I go away that I may come again."

Meanwhile, let the disciple who seeks the renewal of himself learn his relations to the personal and living Saviour, — not merely the Christ of history, who "set an example" to men two thousand years ago, but the Mediator of the ever-present hour, out of whose glorified humanity comes that Divine suffusion whose baptism is unto life eternal. And when he hears a gentle voice, that calls him in accents more deeply moving than he is wont to hear, let him "turn and look," and he will behold one "like unto the Son of Man."

CHAPTER IX.

GETHSEMANE.

"To put on clouds instead of light,
  And cloath the morning-starre with dust,
Was a translation of such height,
  As, but in thee, was ne'er exprest.

"Ah, my dear Lord! what couldst thou spye
  In this impure rebellious clay,
That made thee thus resolve to dye
  For those that kill thee every day?

"O, what strange wonders could thee move
  To slight thy precious bloud and breath?
Sure it was *Love*, my Lord; for Love
  Is only stronger far than death."

VAUGHAN.

It will doubtless occur to the reader, that the foregoing argument is not complete. It will not be forgotten that the Saviour was tempted in all respects as we are, and if temptation can arise only from indwelling evil, how could it occur to him who was the impersonation of Unsullied Purity?

We recur to the distinction, already, we trust, made sufficiently broad and clear, between *sin* and innate *proclivities* to sin. For the first we are guilty, — for the last, never, till they have passed into voluntary action. Those who ignore this distinction, and make "sin a nature," fixing moral guilt upon innate proclivities, may well bring their speculations to a pause in view of the temptations of the desert and Gethsemane. In that presence we file our denial of a theology, which not only contradicts the moral sentiment of mankind, but in its last logical sequence would bring an imputation upon the Divine Sufferer himself. There can be no temptation, without inhering proclivities to wrong. If *they* are sin, what mean the temptations of the Son of Man?

They are not sin. But we go further than this. There may be a case, where to be tempted implies not only the absence of sin, but the highest goodness and mercy; for it may be a means of securing the weak and the fallen from moral ruin.

Suppose a fire to occur at midnight, when some helpless family wakes up and finds itself surrounded with crackling timbers. Kind neighbors assemble. They beckon to the sufferers to come forth. They speak words of encouragement and sympathy. But what does all this avail? for the distracted parents have retreated with their little ones to the last spot which is unconsumed, and while the fire begins to eat upon their flesh, they send forth in vain their cries for deliverance. At that moment the crowd, whose terrified faces reflect the glare that is flung over them, part asunder, and some being, in the calm strength of mercy, walks through the blaze, and, while the flames like the tongues of demons are darting around him, leads forth the family unharmed from their falling habitation. Which was the good man, he who stood aloof with kind words and wishes, or he who came into the actual condition of the sufferers, that he might be their saviour and deliverer? Doubtless the latter.

An angel might have descended from heaven and proclaimed the gospel message from the tops of the mountains, and then returned and beckoned us after him to the skies. We should have gazed after him into heaven, and mused awhile upon the beautiful vision, which would have had no more effect in accomplishing our deliverance, than a remembered dream. We are not angels, and how could we follow him in his flight? This natural man we dwell in had become inflamed with every desire and passion that could destroy the soul. Then Jesus Christ assumed this very nature, with all its cumulative evil, — came down into our fleshly habitation and dwelt in it, that he might deliver us out of it unharmed. He took on him the seed of Abraham, that he might feel all the temptations which we do, and conquer them, — take up all our experience into his, and place upon himself all the burdens of our humanity. "He placed his shoulder beneath the rushing ruin, that he might lift it up into its eternal rest."

And how does Christ deliver us by thus assuming our nature and being touched with the feeling of our infirmities? In two ways.

Here first comes in all the efficacy which we ascribe to the example of the Saviour. It were no example to us, no revelation of *human* perfection, unless it exhibited to us human nature under temptation and suffering, which have so large a place in our earthly probation. We want a pure and perfect ideal, shining aloft like a guiding star, that we may know in what *direction* we are to go. We might strive ever so much after perfection, but we should strive blindly, unless the lost ideal were restored to us. We want not only strength to walk firm, but light to show the way; and hence we look to Christ that we may "follow him in the regeneration." By assuming our nature, he became conscious of all the propensities to wrong that assail us, and by resisting these in his own person till they were slain and banished, his nature was glorified till all its powers were the perfect media of the indwelling Divinity. This is a heaven-drawn picture of our regeneration. We resist the lower, or rather the outward nature, with its hereditary corruptions, till those corruptions cease to be, and then the outward man, instead of being opposed to the inward, becomes the clear medium through which its pure energies are manifested and poured abroad.

The same conflict was in him that there is in us,— and when the conflict ceased he could say, "I and my Father are one"; "Now is the Son of Man glorified, and God is glorified in him";—for then his humanity transmitted only the Holy Spirit, and was the unimpeded forth-going of the Godhead. So in his follower when regenerated,—the whole outward man mirrors forth unclouded the graces of the inhabiting angel.

Again, there is no reason to doubt that these scenes of temptation and suffering prepared him for the grand work of Mediation which we have already described. The influence which comes to us now out of his glorified nature, is adapted tenderly and effectively to our various needs, because he has risen out of this same condition, and can hold communion with us in every stage of our progress. He was not *a* man, but *The Man*. His is the all-comprehensive humanity. What but sin can come into our experience, which his experience has not embraced and taken up? Infancy with all its infolded germs, and manhood with all its conscious proclivities, are here included.

Out of a humanity, therefore, full-orbed and entire, the Comforter now comes to man. And all the Bethlehems, the deserts, the Gethsemanes, and the Calvarys of human life, are spanned by its warmth and effulgence. All conditions, from birth to death, have the Divine aid diversified and meted out to them. All experiences, from the lowest to the highest, have the Divine strength brought home to them in its tender and infinite adaptations. In that he hath "suffered, being tempted, he is able to succor them that are tempted"; and hence the omnipresence of a Saviour's love, that *finds* us from the first inspiration of our infant breath to its last expiration in the gasp of dissolution. If God were to approach us in his unveiled and awful essence, we should perish in the blinding and consuming splendors. But coming to us out of the Glorified Sufferer, we receive of his fulness, grace for his grace, virtue answering to his virtue, till the sweet image of the Crucified has copied itself into our lowly and obedient souls.

CHAPTER X.

THE ATONEMENT.

"And lyke as he made the Jewes and Gentiles *at one* betwene themselves, euen so he made them both *at one* with God, that there should be nothing to breake the *Atonement*, but that the thinges in heauen and the thynges in earth shoulde be ioyned together as it were into *one* body." — UDAL. EPH. c. 2.

WE have partly anticipated this topic in the last two chapters. But the word *Atonement*, though not the one under which the Scriptures usually describe the work of human redemption, has become so prominent in Christian literature, and invested with such peculiar interest, that we do not feel that our statement is exhaustive until the argument has embraced this topic as it lies in our church theologies. We shall note here the various aspects of opinion which this phraseology is supposed to indicate. We do this, not for the sake of controversy, but for the sake of perspicuity. We shall thus accept and appropriate all the truth which this phraseology may symbolize, and we shall make our own doctrine clearly defined and understood. Very likely we may not state these forms of belief with the sharp precision with which they are drawn out in systems of dogmatic theology, which we have not time nor wish now to turn over. We shall state them, however, as we have met them, and as we suppose they lie practically in believing minds.

The atonement is reconciliation of man to God. Two things are implied by this word; first, the final results which the atonement would effectuate, and, secondly, the modes and procedures by which these results are sought. One refers to the end, the other to the means employed.

On the first point we do not know that there is any diversity of opinion, at least any that is worth our analysis. The design of God in the great plan of redemption is to make man holy. Its last results, then, are in the human soul. They are entirely subjective. When human nature is raised up and purified, and brought into harmonic relations with the Divine nature, the final results of the Divine plan are accomplished. It is very true, that there is a great deal of phraseology among theological writers which would fairly imply that the atonement wrought a change in God as well as man, in that it made him placable and "cooled his wrath"; but we presume that these are ideas which all intelligent believers would now disavow. God is unchangeable love and justice, and the only change sought is subjectively in man, so as to bring him within the scope of that love and justice.

But when we come to ask what are the modes and procedures by which God seeks to effect this change in man, we find a diversity of speculations and theories. They may be reduced, however, to four, and be characterized with sufficient precision as the theory of *substitution*, of *exhibition*, of *satisfaction*, and of *mediation*.

1. That of substitution supposes that Christ suffered strictly and literally *in the stead of man*. The law of God denounces eternal misery against sin, even to the smallest transgression. But all men have sinned, and the execution of the law upon them would consign the whole race to hopeless ruin. Then Christ comes as a substitute, and bears in his own person an amount of suffering equivalent to the eternal punishment of all mankind.

But all mankind are not therefore saved. Each has something to do individually in order to appropriate to himself the benefits of this provision. He receives them by an act of faith in this vicarious atonement, whereby all his sins are cancelled.

We reject all this as the plan of system-builders, but not of God. We reject it primarily on Scripture ground, since the original terms from which our word *atonement* comes do not include the notion of vicarious substitution.* That our sins were made over to Christ and his merits made over to us, so that the account may stand balanced in the book of

* The Hebrew verb כפר (Kapher), *to atone*, and its Greek correlates ἱλάσκομαι, ἐξιλάομαι, and καταλλάσσω, mean properly *to produce agreement*. The lexicographers include "to appease" within the import of the first two, but the element of vicarious substitution is totally wanting. See Gen. xxxii. 20; Ex. xxx. 12; Ezek. xvi. 63; xlv. 15; Dan. ix. 24; Is. xxii. 14; Rom. v. 11; 2 Cor. v. 18–20; Eph. ii. 16; Col. i. 20; Heb. ii. 17; Matt. v. 24.

doom, are notions which we hold to be remnants of scholastic web-weaving, having no basis in Scripture or in the nature of things. How Christ "takes our infirmities and bears our sicknesses" will be quite obvious by reference to the language of the Evangelist in Matthew viii. 17. What he did for man physically illustrates what he was doing for man spiritually. He did not cure the leper by becoming one himself, thus drawing off the disease into his own person; he cured him by cleansing the leprosy away.

But, again, there is no economy in this plan. The design of infinite mercy is the prevention of suffering in the universe. But under this scheme no suffering has been saved. Just as great an amount has transpired as if Christ had never come, and the whole race been doomed to eternal woe. All that woe was concentred on him, who was "surrounded, and, as it were, besieged with an army of sorrows." The storm has had its way, and spent all its rage, and effected all its ruin, only the scene of ruin was transferred to another field. But there it is, and there it lies, an equal space of blackness and desolation in the fair universe of God. The punishment has fallen in all its weight, and produced all its pangs, only it has taken a different direction. All the difference is this, — that the guilty who deserved it would otherwise have borne it, whereas the innocent that did not deserve it bears it now! No matter, in the light of this argument, whether the innocent were a willing victim or not. Such a scheme of mercy has prevented no suffering, nor saved the universe a single pang.

"But this plan is the only one that can produce holiness." In other phrase, they alone whose faith takes this special and technical form are holy. The assumption means that, if it means any thing, and it is quite as inconsistent with the known facts of history as with a comprehending charity. Charity is the prime essential of salvation, and it is not apt to coexist very long with that exclusive spirit which comes from making belief in dogmas the separating line of human character.

So, again, we reject this theory, because of the adjuncts which it draws along with it, and which no logic that we are masters of can clear away. It makes salvation depend on the accidents of birth, locality, and position. All who lived before Christ are lost, for no such atonement was preached to them. The Jews even, who believed prospectively in Christ, believed in him not as a suffering Messiah, and elaborated no such theory as this from their own Scripture. All who live outside of Christendom are lost, for they never heard of this atonement, and could not be saved by believing it. Alas for the sages and good men who lived by the light of nature as well as they might, and the record of whose virtues so often flings shame upon our Christian practice! For four thousand years the world was a mistake, and man a failure, and with few exceptions he is a failure yet. All who die before the age of rationality are lost, for without rationality they cannot grasp such a faith; and so infancy and childhood go down in a hopeless procession into that folding night which the fingers of morning are never to unbar. Most who die within Christendom are lost, including the vast numbers of humble and pious men and women who never theologize, but simply trust in Christ and there leave the matter, and thence build their hope in heaven, — but in vain. We dread the influence of these ideas on our worship, for they darken our thought of God; on our charity, for they hedge it in and destroy all large, genial, and goodly fellowship; on our preparation for a better state, for they make faith, and not life, primary and fundamental.*

2. The second theory supposes it necessary that God should make such an *exhibition* to the universe of his displeasure against sin, that men would be impressed with the idea of its deadly nature. Such an exhibition was the scene on Calvary. Forgiveness on simple repentance were not otherwise safe.

---

* We do not mean to say, that all these dismal consequences are acknowledged and embraced by all who hold the doctrine of a vicarious atonement. But admitting that the end of the atonement is to produce a change not in God, but in man, we say these consequences are the necessary corollaries of the theory of substitution. For the matter stands thus: —

A vicarious atonement by the death of Christ was not necessary to prevent suffering, for the whole equivalent suffering has transpired.

It was not necessary to salvation, if human beings are saved without believing it.

If they are not saved without believing it, then all the adjuncts belong to it which the text details.

They would sin again and again, if they thought forgiveness were so cheaply obtained. Not so when they look at the great agony on Calvary, where they see at once the cost of forgiveness and the frown of God upon transgression.

We lay off from all this so much as would impute to God the work of scene-showing for the sake of sensible impression, if such a conception be included, and then we come to the essential truth which this theory contains. The cross *is*, in a most important sense, the expression of God's hatred of sin. There is the point where the awful antagony between the eternal purity and human corruption was even brought down into the sphere of sense and made apprehensible there. Would the Son of God become incarnate and surround himself with the lowly conditions of mortal existence, would such a being suffer and die, would all this wealth of means be expended to banish sin from the domains of God, unless he regarded it as the supreme curse, the infinite woe? The sinner may, indeed, measure the depth of his guilt by the height of that great agony. But let him not look to Calvary as the place of scenic display. Rather were the agony and the darkened sun the ultimation on the plane of nature of the state of fallen humanity. The Jewish Church was darkened, she on whom the Everlasting Light arose. Her sun was blotted out, and her stars had fallen from the sky. Her children had committed that sin which is called unpardonable. They had been guilty of the awful crime of Deicide, for they had killed the Divine Life in the soul, and in the Church God's mystical body. Let this spiritual state be outshadowed in the visible world and on the plane of nature, and there culminate in its last results, and what else would they be, what else *could* they be, but the sun gone out in the heavens, and that form which was the incarnation of the Divine Life hung bleeding upon the cross, or laid in the sepulchre stiff and cold? It is a mistake to imagine that here is an exhibition of the nature of Jewish sin in particular, and not of all sin, ever and everywhere. All sin is a conflict with the Divine nature, only here the scene of that conflict was outshadowed from the field of spirit into the field of sense. The Divine Life is first resisted and crucified within, and after that we are in opposition to all its embodiments without, and if in our power we should resist and crucify it there. The cause of eternal truth and right, God's ever-returning and reappearing Messiah, has always waked up the same conflict as it comes athwart the lusts of selfish men, and every country has its bloody Calvary and its holy sepulchre where that truth was murdered and entombed. On all the high places of the earth has the Christ been slain. In Judea he appeared in human form and with more intimate relations with nature, and so there nature was afflicted and shaken when the sacrifice was made. It would be so again could there be such a thing as a reincarnation of the Word. It is the essential opposition between an unregenerate human nature, with its cruel lusts and passions, and the Divine nature so pure and awfully serene. The denial, the conflict, and the *Deicidium* commence in the secret soul. Their forth-going and culmination are seen in the awful spectacle on Calvary.

We must not imagine, however, that impressions from without upon the senses are chiefly efficacious in making forgiveness safe or sin hateful. When God comes within us and reveals us, and shows our inhering corruption in contrast with the eternal purity and holiness, we have an exhibition of the hatefulness of sin, such as no spectacle in the natural world can give. It is the everlasting light let down through the abysses of our being, detecting sin in all its hiding-places, and unveiling its intrinsic qualities to the afflicted consciousness. Whoever has attained to regeneration, forgiveness, and peace, through these self-explorations (and forgiveness comes in no other way), no more desires to relapse into his former state, than the prisoner who has emerged out of the miasma of a noisome dungeon into the blessed light and air, desires to be remanded to his prison again. "They would sin again and again, if they thought repentance were so easily obtained." As if the new man could regard sin as the supreme good, be drawn to it by all his interior sympathies, and only serve God under *duress* and be bound to that service by galling chains!

3. The third theory supposes that in some way the Divine law was satisfied by Jesus Christ, so as to render it possible for God to pardon sin; and this

we have called the theory of satisfaction. It does not assert that the sufferings of Christ were strictly vicarious; but it does assert, that Christ in some way satisfied the demands of the law, preserved its honor and integrity, so that now men can be saved on condition of repentance; whereas if Christ had not died, repentance would have been unavailing.

All this we hold. But we must explain more fully what we understand by the Divine law, in order to evolve whatever of truth this formula of doctrine may contain.

By law we may mean either of two things. We may mean those principles of eternal order according to which the Divine Mind always operates, and the Divine energies always flow. These principles pervade all modes of being, spirit and matter, the spirit world and the natural. They constitute that law which Hooker defines so well, "whose seat is the bosom of God, and whose voice is the harmony of the world." By this the worlds are formed, for they are the emanations of the Eternal Energy shaped by the Eternal Reason, "without which nothing was made that was made." They are the Divine Word in action, constituting that inmost life of things which determines all form and motion, and is ever in effort to shape and guide them so as to express and copy out the Divine idea of the supreme excellency and beauty. "The speech of God which produces the works of creation is the immutable reason, not a sound spoken and vanishing, but a force eternally subsisting and flowing through nature."* The method by which this force always flows is the Divine law, for it is the method of Divine action. It is the SUPREME ORDER, which God cannot break, and which if man breaks, he surely suffers. In accordance with this same truth, the Greek called the creation the Cosmos, or Beautiful Order.

Or, again, we may mean by the Divine law these inhering and pervading principles described and embodied in a written code. But this is all the same, except that now the law that ever works in the heart and substance of things is put into the formulas of language. Divine revelation is a disclosure to man of those immutable principles according to which the spirit-world is arranged; for man had lost the intuitive knowledge of these in his degeneracy and fall. In other phrase, the Divine Word, by which all things are made, whose eternal forth-goings constitute the inmost life of angel, spirit, or man, and whose lowest revealments and blossomings constitute the natural world with all its outspread scenery, is clothed in the symbols of speech, and that gives us the Bible or written word; but clothed in nature, or clothed in language, its established sequences or its order of operation is the perfect and everlasting law.

All this is very clear. But we illustrate further.

---

* "Dei quippe sublimor ante suum factum locutio ipsius sui facti est immutabilis ratio, quæ non habet sonum strepentem atque transeuntem, sed vim sempiterne manentem et temporaliter operantem." — Augustine, *De Civ. Dei.*

It is a law of nature that matter gravitates towards matter, a law pervading primarily every atom and thence every world, making planets and suns travel the fields of space according to a divine arrangement, and thus unrolling in its order the scenery of the skies. It was well for man to know this law; but his knowing it did not make it, and does not alter it. It was all the same before put into the formulas of Newton's Principia. Again, it is a law of the spirit-world that love unifies and draws together, and hate repels and puts asunder; that one places the soul in harmony with the Divine nature, and so draws it to God, and that the other places it in opposition, so that the Divine nature repels it. This law, operating first in individual minds and thence in the social and spiritual worlds, arranges the vast scheme of existence through all its descending grades and orders, from the blessed spirits who "all day long bask round the throne of God," to those who seek the abysses of night, away from the Divine countenance because they "hate its beams." This law creates and arranges heaven and hell. This ever was and ever must be. And when revelation placed before us the words, Come, ye blessed! and Depart, ye cursed! it put into its formula a law of eternal order.

When written laws are not the exposition of inworking and unchanging principles, we call them *arbitrary*. They are something superimposed. They are forced upon us by a foreign will, a will painfully dissonant from that whose voice is the harmony of the worlds. They are not transcripts of the unchangeable Justice. Hence, though man's laws may be arbitrary, God's never can be. He never can put into a written code, for man's observance, aught else than the principles of the Beautiful Order. The previous law was perfect, for it was God's inworking and perfect will. God is wise, and cannot err in the transcript. He will transcribe none other, for he will not act in opposition to himself or in discordance with his own will.

Now we fully believe and hold that the race could not be redeemed, and the supreme order remain unbroken, without the incarnation, death, and resurrection of the Son of Man. These are all the fulfilment of the everlasting law, — not of an arbitrary rule of Divine action, but of principles that inhere in the constitution of the universe. Could we see things from that point whence the omniscient eye surveys them, looking from centre to circumference, we should see, doubtless, why God could not otherwise impart himself to humanity so as to regenerate and save it. We should see that there was no other mode of the Divine advent, without some infraction of that law whose voice is the universal harmony. Even with our low and finite views, we can see some of the reasons why this is so. For suppose God had been revealed to darkened and fallen man, not through a humanity that came down into man's condition, but out of the naked heavens and in his unclothed and burning essence, how might man's free agency have been destroyed, while God became to him a blasting light or a consuming fire! Or suppose God had imparted himself by an influent life, which human nature weak and palsied by sin could not bear; how might man have moved under a power that overlaid his volitions and possessed his faculties, and so have been merged in passive nature, and ceased to be man! Hence we say and believe, that not only the death of Christ, but the incarnation, with all its concomitants, the radiating fact in human history, to which all fore-time and after-time have reference, is a fulfilment of the eternal law, the perfection and preservation of the Beautiful Order.*

4. The pernicious consequence of framing a theory of the atonement which shall be dominant and exclusive, must, we think, be obvious. In any single view of this central fact, we get only one of its benignant aspects, — and it is proof enough that this is a Divine work, that no one theory which men have framed about it is exhaustive or comprehends it. It will be seen at once, that the views presented under the last head pertain more to the reasons and motives of Divine action, than to the positive duties

* We have heard it said, "How are our past sins to be cancelled, without a vicarious atonement? Even could we become perfectly holy, there is the unsatisfied law claiming vengeance for the guilty past." As if God's law were arbitrary, a mere parchment regulation, that requires vengeance to be rained upon us from without, after we have been brought into inward harmony with the Divine will! Since the law is none other than the Divine nature acting within us, it is satisfied when it has brought our natures into entire concord with itself, and never till then. After that, punishment for the past would be revenge.

of man. The sinner may receive all the benefits of the atonement, without knowing all the reasons and motives of it. We come, then, to another theory, that of mediation, not as distinct from the last two, but including them and a great deal more. It does not attempt to scan this great work from the Divine point of view, but to present it to man in its practical bearing, and thus to turn its full power upon the human soul.

We have already attempted to describe the atonement in this bearing and aspect, in the last two chapters. It offers to us Jesus Christ as the medium of Divine truth, and of that sovereign energy under which man is created anew and restored to God's resplendent image. It seeks less to explore the processes by which this is done, or the reasons which necessitate this mode of Divine operation. Enough that God is in Christ, reconciling the world unto himself, and that those who yield themselves to him have their natures restored to heavenly order and peace, and are drawn to God in relations that are sweet and tender. It is this which meets the wants of man as a sinner. It is this which has saved thousands who never elaborated a philosophy of salvation. Profoundly acknowledging the Messiahship of Christ and his indwelling Divinity, and brought in meek surrender at his feet, they find themselves ensphered by the power of the Godhead, whereby they change from sin to holiness; and health runs through their whole spiritual frames; the palsied powers are touched and lifted up; the

Adam of consciousness is expelled, and the Christ of consciousness is formed out of the old chaos; a new creation beneath the eye of God, "how good, how fair, answering his great idea." This, in a most important sense, is being clothed in the righteousness of Christ, not by a factitious transfer of his righteousness to our account, but by his life imported into our natures, and thence going out into conduct. It is a righteousness not imputed, but imparted. This is the essential work of the atonement, and in this wise it lies in the inmost consciousness of all true and humble believers. They know that God in Christ is brought near to them, and folds them in his renewing light and love. That God in imparting himself through such a Mediator fulfils his own eternal law, they doubt not; their part is to be brought into such relation to Christ, that his imparted life shall be the prompting of all their affections and powers. This is the atonement, we say, as it lies at the centre of the Christian consciousness, and as such it appears conspicuously in the first conversions to Christianity. It was God in Christ, coming anew into the heart of humanity and making conquest of all its powers, striking down the persecutor with shafts of light, and swaying vast multitudes, because on them "the Holy Ghost fell." This relation to a Divine Mediator is cognizable in the intuitions of all pious men; it has inspired every thing in Christian literature that speaks to our inmost needs, and all that truly lives in its sacred songs. Sinful man, by a lowly surrender of himself to Christ, brought into dear and harmonic relations with the Divine nature, — this is the fact of the atonement, whatever be its philosophy. The fact cannot be reasoned out of the true believer, for it belongs to his intuitive consciousness. To account for it, to draw it out in schemes of theology, and give the reasons of the Divine plan, is a process of logic alone. This last process may lead into mazes and errors, for logic does not create truth, nor see it in its source, but seeks rather to hammer its broken ore into shapes for convenient handling. With our intuitive consciousness it is otherwise; for with it we are brought face to face with truth in its living source, and gaze with open eye on its supreme excellences and glories.

It will hence appear what is the peculiar efficacy of *faith* in the salvation of man, which the New Testament writers make so much account of, and on which Paul, especially, insists so largely. It is not merely a belief in any amount of dogmas and postulates, however true. It is not merely a belief in Christ as an authorized teacher of religion and morals. It is such belief as shall lead to an all-confiding trust. Trust is the more appropriate word; for the faith in Christ that saves, is not so much the result of intellection as a perception of his moral grandeur and Divinity, adequate to our necessities, and adapted to fill the chasm in our natures. Then we fly to him with the swift alacrity of a child that seeks a lost parent, and our natures are tender and pliable beneath his hand. Faith in Christ is not a mere belief in the historical advent, but in the living Christ that ever comes from the heavens as the Comforter and Redeemer of souls. Such was the faith for which Paul reasoned so earnestly; not a faith which should entitle the believer to a share in some reserved fund of foreign merit, but bring him into living relations to a Divine Mediator, so that his heart should be swept all the while with renewing gales, and have a righteousness imparted to him every hour. Precisely here is the point where he contrasts the dead works of the ceremonial law with the works of faith under Christianity. *They* were the righteousness of the outward man. *These* were the outgoings, the outburstings, shall we not say, of the life whose unfailing tides came in upon them in consequence of their relation to a living Intercessor in the heavens. Paul himself had had a signal experience of this influence, melting the adamant of Jewish bigotry, and making the Pharisee as humble as a child, while the source of this influence was unveiled to him in its insufferable splendors. Hence his great topic is faith in Christ, as the essential of inward life and power; the essential of that regenerating influence which should draw man to God, and so restore human nature and the Divine nature to their primal harmonies. "One Mediator, Christ," says old Tyndal, "and by that word vnderstand an *attonemaker*, a peace-maker, and brynger into grace and fauour, hauyng full power to do so."

CHAPTER XI.

NEW HEAVENS AND A NEW EARTH.

"What this repentance was which the new covenant required as one of the conditions to be performed by all those who should receive the benefits of that covenant, is plain in the Scripture to be not only sorrow for sins past, but (what is a natural consequence of such sorrow if it be real) a turning from them into a new and contrary life." — LOCKE'S REASONABLENESS OF CHRISTIANITY.

"Work! and thou shalt bless the day
Ere thy task be done;
They that work not, cannot pray,
Cannot feel the sun.

"Worlds thou mayst possess with health
And unslumbering powers;
Industry alone is wealth, —
What we do is ours."

THERE is a state of mind which we call *repentance*, — the antecedent of regeneration and permanent peace, whose nature it behooves us well to understand. Whenever the book of life within us is unfolded, and the Divine light falls upon its open pages, we see and feel the afflicting contrast between that life and the all-perfect law. The immanence of God in unregenerate man brings to view at length the all-holy and pure in contrast with human corruption. Then sin and the corrupt fountains of sin appear to us more hideous than death, not merely for the inconveniences that will follow after them, but on account of their own intrinsic nature. Nothing, then, appears to us so dreadful to be borne, as the present burden of moral disease; and we shall pray for its removal more earnestly than we would pray for the extraction of a cancer from our vitals. The affliction which we experience from the unveiling of inherent corruption, is what the Scriptures describe under the phrase "godly sorrow." It is not regret on account of the consequences of sin, but an afflicting consciousness of its nature. The change of life prompted by this state of mind the Scriptures call REPENTANCE.*

Hence an all-important distinction. Neither sorrow nor emotion of any kind is true repentance. Godly sorrow precedes and prompts it, but there may be godly sorrow even without it. Our translators have unfortunately rendered by the same word two others, which stand for very different ideas. One word implies simply sorrow for the past; the other implies sorrow for the past consummated in a new life. One is mental emotion. The other is mental emotion invested with new moralities. One (μετάμελος) is sorrow of mind, and is used to describe the emotions of Judas before he hanged himself.† The other (μετάνοια) is change of purpose and conduct, and describes that repentance over which the angels rejoice as they bend around the

* 2 Cor. vii. 9, 10. † Matt. xxvii. 3.

returning prodigal to breathe over him his welcome home.*

Two worlds are ours, one creative of the other. There is the inner realm of thought, emotion, and imagination, and there is the outward realm of practice, where thought, emotion, and imagination take their investiture of flesh and matter, and pass into nature and history. In one we have them in their warmth and fusion, in the other we have them crystallized into fact. All radical changes in character begin with changes in the inner realm of thought and emotion. There we are moved upon by the powers that are above us; by the Eternal Spirit that lies on our souls like a haunting presence, giving us visions of celestial purity, bitter compunctions, sighs for a better state, and images that float down out of heaven through our fancies. But none of these are yet ours. They sometimes come without any agency whatever of our own. Thus far they have wrought no change in character, for they have not yet passed under the action of a human will. Left to themselves they are indeterminate as celestial ethers. They are appropriated by a distinct agency on our part, which consists in giving them a place by our own right arm among fixed and solid realities. The thoughts and emotions wrought in us by the Spirit of God are as yet foreign to us. They are heavenly treasures let down within our grasp. We grasp them by fixing them

* Luke xv. 10.

in the voluntary life, and then they are for ever ours.

The words *heaven* and *earth* are employed by the sacred writers to describe this twofold realm of inward faith and feeling, and outward life and practice. For heaven is the higher state of being, and earth is the world of grosser substances. Things seen are the copies and manifestations of things invisible. So heaven and earth, in the figurative language of Scripture, mean, first, that supernal state into which man's mind may be elevated, and whence it may be impressed and moved, and, again, that external sphere of action into which this state passes by his free volitions and energies; one a counterpart of the other; the last imprinted by the first and receiving and fixing its ideals.*

Or, to insist on a still more literal and scientific exposition of the terms, earth is none other than the atmospheres of heaven arrested and condensed into solid forms. The ethers that expand above us through infinite depths of blue, through which float the amber clouds or stream the glories of a firmament of suns, are simply what remains of those atmospheres that determined into shape and became the earths of a beneficent and ever-working system.

---

* For instances where the word *heaven* is used representatively for the highest or inmost principles and truths, and *earth* for those principles and truths embodied in grosser forms, in the external life, in institutions religious and civil, see Is. xiii. 13; xxxiv. 4; lxv. 17; lxvi. 22; Luke iii. 21; xxi. 26; John i. 51; iii. 13; Acts ii. 19, 20; Col. i. 20; Rev. xxi. 1.

Even thus the new heaven of truth that opens upon us, and the celestial ethers that play upon our souls, are arrested and made permanent by being turned into new moralities. Out of the new heavens that God provides, the new earth is formed, — and then man is a new creation, a microcosm in which all spiritual and earthly things are abridged and pictured forth.

From this exposition of the nature of repentance, a lesson comes to us which is most important and solemn. There is a constant tendency in the unregenerate heart, to seek some substitute for the new creation, in obtaining Divine favor and pardon. Sometimes it is a mystic faith, sometimes it is mystic emotion, but all ending short of new moralities. Hence the pernicious habit of delay in religion, under the delusive idea that the regenerate man is a sudden and miraculous creation out of nothing, never considering, that not only a new heaven is to be created, but also "a new earth in which dwelleth righteousness." There is a class of mental exercises known as "death-bed repentances," the nature and efficacy of which may now be pretty clearly distinguished. We know, for we have seen, the spiritualizing influence of sickness upon the heart and character. We have stood by the bed of death, when the spirit seemed unclothed gradually and gently, as by an angel's softest touch, and finally passed away like a wave scarcely breaking upon the immortal shores. But what we now refer to is the sudden and radical change that is supposed to take place in impenitent men who have postponed the claims of God and the angel-call, when thought and feeling are deemed a sufficient equivalent for a new life. It is evident enough that even godly sorrow could not now become repentance. Character can no more be built on thought and feeling, than a house can be built on air. Prayer may be fervent, but prayer at that hour can only be spoken, not acted. Penitence may be deep, but it cannot be turned into fact Truth may be contemplated, but it cannot crystallize into conduct. Good purposes may be formed, but they cannot go into execution. Once the feet might have moved swift on the errands of love, once the hand was strong to do its work. But the feet will not now bear up their load, and "the graceful right hand has lost its cunning." God may bend over him the new heavens, from which shine the eternal stars, and may breathe around him celestial ethers that play into his heart, but the new earth cannot now be formed out of them, and without both no man is a new creation. So that the dying man wakes up unchanged among spiritual realities, his baseless imaginations all vanishing like the fast-fading hues of sunset clouds, when the blackness of night is all that remains. No truth is ours till the arm has given it a local habitation, and no emotion passes into a permanent frame until it determines into principle. No theology is saving that is not worked, no man is in the way to heaven who is not in the way of a good and a useful life. From a disregard of these truths, how many have sought heaven in vain through "imputed righteousness," and how many churches have become dead, and left high and dry on the barren downs, while the stream of history is sweeping by! Faith becomes separated from life, having no connection with week-day affairs, and the Church stands in the midst of society, having no more living relations with its business than the bones that slumber beneath its chancel-floors.

CHAPTER XII.

RETROSPECT AND PROSPECT.

> "Survey the bright dominions
> In the gorgeous colors drest
> Flung from off the purple pinions
> Evening spreads throughout the west!"
>
> WORDSWORTH.

We ask the reader's attention a little further, while we retrace the path we have gone over, and note the distinct stages of Christian progress. Not that these can always be so defined in individual experience, that the point of transition from one to another will be fully marked and distinguished. Nevertheless they are there; and, described in succession, they will be recognized as separate portions of that way over which the pilgrim travels from the "city of Destruction" to the "city of God."

1. First is the decisive act of self-consecration to the Divine Spirit, that speaks in us and claims us from our infant years. The idea of the heavenly life, once received, will glow in the young mind like a live coal, every thing tending to fortify the holy purpose and make it the governing and unitizing principle of all endeavor. Happy are they who have early embraced this idea, and who, in the first joy-

ous exercise of the dawning reason, have not been disobedient to the heavenly vision. They preserve their youthful virtue "englobed" within them, never yielding to depraved hereditary impulsions, not listening to the voice of false charmers, but to the "COME UP HITHER" of the angel powers. The first exercise of the high prerogatives of free moral agency is thus the first stage in a life of holiness. It is the first decisive CHOICE between hereditary or surrounding evil that sways us towards the world of shadows, and the God that ever knocketh at the door of our hearts and calleth us to the world of light.

2. Those who have chosen the good and the true, and the life in conformity with them, sometimes fondly imagine that naught lies before them now but a path of roses. They think the Christian life is only an easy progress from one pleasant prospect to another. But they find they are mistaken. They did not know all that was in them at the beginning. But the God to whom they have consecrated themselves, the Light which they have chosen to follow, is sure to reveal them. He comes within them when invoked and welcomed, first to pour a startling radiance through their disordered nature, and make all its hidden corruption stand confessed. To this end is the discipline of life, to this end the allurements of temptation, to this end all trials and sufferings, — God's heralds of mercy in rough disguise, — to this end at first his holy word, that holds to human nature an unerring glass. Thus our most secret foes

come out of their ambush and file before us in dark array till our SELF-REVELATION is complete.

3. Then comes the battle of life. Then we understand what the old saints mean, who call the Christian life a life of struggle and warfare. We seem, it may be, to have backslidden from our position, when we embraced in our first enthusiasm the idea of the Christian life; and the blessed prospect that rose on our earlier vision is snatched from view. At the season of our baptismal vows, the heavens were opening and the Holy Dove descending. That has passed away like a dream of paradise, and we find ourselves on the desert of temptation in conflict with its beasts of prey. Our deepest want is now felt; all human aid is utterly insufficient; mere examples and models of perfection mock and afflict us, for we cannot reach them; the teachings of conflicting sects grate on our ears like Babel-noises; we see away and above us the land of peace, but, hedged about with foes, we cannot travel its upward path, while

> "Rooted here we stand, and gaze
> On those bright steps that heavenward raise
> Their practicable way."

Such is the region where lies the CONFLICT OF LIFE, when our weakness is felt most despairingly, and we fling away as worthless our broken shield.

4. Then the want within us points to Him who alone can save. The Mediator, from whom comes to us the all-revealing and renewing Divinity, rises on our sight, as he rose on his early Church, like the

sun shining in his strength. If before he was only a teacher and an example, he is now a quickening and regenerating power. If before we were comfortless and desolate, yet basking in the clear blaze of his Divinity, the Comforter falls on our souls like showers of morning light. If before we trusted to the barren technicologies of schools and sects, they now melt away like web-work before this bright coming of the Lord. If before we trusted to a righteousness imputed, we now rejoice in a righteousness imparted every hour. If then we were only conscious of indwelling sin, we now become daily conscious of the indwelling Christ. If God before had been to us only as an "abstraction" and a "principle," whom prayer could not reach or bring down from the yielding heavens, call loudly as we might, he is now brought near to us in a Mediator that ever floods his Church, his body of true believers, with light and love. A new heaven has opened above us, whence falls the everlasting light, and whence comes the blessed ventilation of renewing gales. Thus we "receive the ATONEMENT."

5. And yet all these heavenly frames of mind might pass away, and these tender communings might grow less and less and cease for ever, did they not prompt us to a new life of action, and give us new delight in doing the Divine will. But Christ thus received seeks a new incarnation in every deed we do. The holy affections wrought within become our permanent possessions, because they are embodied in the daily forth-goings of a Christian life, with all its radiating charities. And since he that doeth

the Divine will shall know of the doctrine, while every revelation prompts to deed, every deed becomes in turn a revelation. So man becomes a new creation, ever rising towards perfection, beneath the hand of the Omnipotent Framer. "I saw a new heaven and a NEW EARTH, for the first heaven and the first earth were passed away."

Not always, not often indeed, does our warfare entirely cease, so that we feel that our day of probation is over and our final heaven has begun. The old lusts and appetites, though they grow weaker and weaker, sometimes awake and renew the conflict, after we thought our final victory had been won. Doubts will arise and becloud our faith, and the prospect that opened so fair upon us dissolves away. But he who lives the life we have described, ascends sometimes those sun-smit summits where the tempters never come, above all cares and troubles, above even the clouds and the thunders, where he catches the fore-gleams of the land of peace and has the earnest of its blissful rest. There are those who, while yet enrobed with mortality, have reached these golden heights never to descend from them, never more to be tempted by sin, never more to be perplexed with doubt, whose placid affections are never ruffled, but rise in perpetual prayer, and on whose ears the sounds from the world they have overcome rise like murmurs from a land afar. Such is entire regeneration. If we follow Christ in the regeneration, and are faithful unto the end, death may find us at that peaceful summit of the western hills.

CHAPTER XIII.

VISTAS.

"For brass I will bring gold, and for iron I will bring silver, and for wood brass, and for stones iron." — ISAIAH lx. 17.

WE revert to the law of descent, so clearly and forcibly unfolded by the Apostle, the law through whose operation come both the fall and the restoration of man. In running out the parallel between Adam and Christ, he makes the blessing commensurate with the bane. Through the first all die, for the foul tides of a perverted ancestral life flow on with ever-fresh accumulations of moral disease: through the last shall all be made alive, because the new life imparted by Jesus Christ is also transmissive, gathering power and intensity with every age, and becoming the richest inheritance of man. This is waxing while the other is waning. Hence a LAW OF PROGRESS made operative by Christianity, which in time is sure to renovate the world. While the work of individual regeneration is going on, the work of social and humanitary regeneration is proceeding at the same time. Not solely, nor yet principally, by conversion and conquest, is Christ to take possession of his kingdom. He comes by a more internal way.

By generic tendencies, that gather purity and volume the farther they extend, the race is advancing, and a "golden progeny" daily descending from heaven. Hereditary evil is to grow less and less, while a pure hereditary life becomes more deep and strong. The regeneration of the individual is measured in its successive stages by the months and years; the regeneration of the race by cycles and centuries. From year to year we may not see the work of progress, but by comparing remote periods we see the melioration of its cruel customs, the gentle infusion of the spirit of mercy, and the extension of the ties of brotherhood from class to class and from people to people, binding together anew a race that had existed so long as portions and fragments of an ancient ruin.

Hence the first essential work of reform is in separate individual minds. We may besiege our social evils from without with ever so much of noise and shouting, but since they are but our inward and perverted life, putting out into leaf and flower, we might tear away the leaves and flowers only to be produced again. Not that reform should not be preached, and Christianity faithfully applied to all outward abuses. But the prime duty of every man, not only to himself and God, but to his race, is self-purification, so that his nature shall be receptive of angelic affections and transmit them as the best inheritance to the coming time. He is no true reformer who does not study as in the fear of God the laws of his own existence, both psychological and physical, and conform to them as laws that are sacred and Divine, deeming the transmission of evil tendencies as the foulest wrong which he can inflict upon his kind. They have done the most for the race whose inheritance to it is a pure and lofty manhood, and from whom the sacred stream of being comes down unpolluted and strong. By such a "transmigration of souls" they become immortal on the earth, and they are abroad on errands of goodness while their bodies moulder in the cerements of the grave.

There is a tradition of the Church founded on obscure prophecy, that Christ is to descend again upon the earth and reign a thousand years. Like the Jewish tradition of the Messiah, we think it has gathered around it human additions by coming through a corrupt past. He came to the Jews in a manner they had nct conceived of, in their dreams of a temporal kingdom; and so his coming again will doubtless transcend the highest thoughts of a sensual age. He comes not from without nor with observation. He hath imported a new element into human history, which is to work there for ever and prevail at length over all other elements. Hidden deep beneath the world's tumult and confusion, it remains secure. Not alone by preachers and apostles and outward means is this new force to prevail. Mark the terms in the two branches of Paul's antithesis: "*As* in Adam all die, *even so* in Christ shall all be made alive." As the Adam of history became the Adam of consciousness, and passed thence into history again and took possession of the world, so the Christ of history becomes the Christ of consciousness, passing again into history till he lights up all its dark and bloody annals. He descends not through the cloven heavens, but through the human soul, in that divine life which grows more full and deep with every new generation, shaping to itself first man's inmost being, and thence flowering forth into the most external affairs, in works of justice and love, until the face of the earth wears again the bloom and the beauty of Eden. Old prophecy describes the reign of Christ as the reign of peace. When he comes within us to disarm and expel our domestic foes, — they of our own spiritual household, — the conflict there is at an end, and the soul is "a dwelling-place for all sweet sounds and harmonies." When this work is everywhere accomplished, there will also be peace without; for society is the manifestation of man's inmost state, the radiation of his most secret life on the face of nature. So when that life is purified, it will fill the world with the trophies of peaceful industry, with the consenting voice of peoples and nations restored to one brotherhood, and with the hosannas of a redeemed humanity that strews the way of the Lord with palms. Not out of the skies, therefore, but out of the depths of human nature renewed and restored, does Christ come to establish his throne on the earth. When the law of descent is restored completely to its beneficent operation, and when it shall send along the future only an enlarging inheritance of good, society and the race, as well as the individual, will be regenerated, or, in Paul's language, "made alive in Christ"; and then the night of centuries brightens into the millennial day.

Sublime, therefore, is the march of generations. The kingdom of Christ will not fail of its triumphs, since Christ not less then Adam has become immanent in humanity. When weary of present evil and surrounding corruption, it is animating sometimes to look away, and in the sure light of Christian truth to watch the lengthening file of years that grow radiant as they run.

THE END.

www.ingramcontent.com/pod-product-compliance
Lightning Source LLC
LaVergne TN
LVHW050514100826
845148LV00002B/328

* 9 7 8 1 4 2 5 5 2 1 7 6 9 *